Let's Celebrate

*A*ren't holidays wonderful? They bring us opportunities to pause in our busy lives and take time for reflection, family togetherness, and just plain fun. The special traditions involving food, music, and decorations that go along with holiday merriment form an ideal basis for many classroom activities. Children learn about the cultures and traditions of their own and other countries via holiday experiences. Be sure to invite community members and families of your students who come from other countries into the classroom to share their own special holiday traditions and beliefs.

Many holidays are religious in origin. If you are not comfortable with religious holidays in the classroom, there are many activities presented in this book that relate to the more secular or seasonal aspects of these holidays. Also, remember that religious holidays can be presented in an educational manner. It is enriching to learn about the beliefs and practices of other people.

A number of American holidays are patriotic in nature. The activities for these holidays are to some extent interchangeable. Likewise, many of the ideas featured under Native American Day can be used at Thanksgiving, which many teachers use to introduce their students to Native American culture.

In this book we have tried to focus on holidays that are most familiar and that bring us together as Americans. The holidays are organized chronologically, beginning with January 1. There are craft activities, recipes, games, and poems—something to celebrate in every month, in every season, throughout the year.

Happy holidays!
Martha Cheney and Brenda Austin

Martha Cheney has taught preschool through fifth grade in both public and private schools. She currently writes children's songs as well as educational materials for school and home use. She is married and the mother of two teenage sons. She and her family live in a mountain valley in western Montana.

Brenda Austin has taught primary-aged children for more than 15 years, both as a classroom teacher and as an on-site environmental educator. She enjoys sharing her love of nature with children and is involved in several literacy programs. She lives in southern California with her husband and children.

New Year's Day

Children usually return to school after New Year's Day, but you can enjoy a belated observance of the holiday. Make sure all children are aware of the New Year. Show the children a calendar. Point out that January 1 is the first date on the calendar.

★ Classroom Resolutions

Explain that the coming of the New Year is a chance for a new start. Give some examples of simple resolutions and explain that they are promises we make to ourselves to improve ourselves or the world around us.

Decide on some simple class resolutions for the New Year, such as helping each other, getting to school on time, or keeping the classroom neat. Write each one on a sentence strip and post. Read them often and use them as encouraging reminders.

★ Good Luck Food

In the southern United States, many people eat black-eyed peas on New Year's Day. It is a tradition that is said to bring good luck. Make black-eyed peas a tradition in your classroom. Corn muffins from a mix or your favorite recipe make a wonderful accompaniment.

Make black-eyed peas:
1. Rinse a bag of dried black-eyed peas and soak them overnight.
2. Place beans in a crock pot, cover with water, and set on high heat.
3. Add a few strips of bacon if desired and some salt and pepper.
4. Beans are ready to eat when soft. Check occasionally and add water if needed. Cooking may take several hours.

To save time, use canned black-eyed peas. Just heat and serve.

Chinese New Year

The date of the Chinese New Year varies because it is based on the ancient and complex Chinese lunar calendar. It is the most important date on the Chinese calendar and is celebrated exuberantly.

The dragon parade is part of the traditional observance of the holiday. The dragon is a symbol of great good to the Chinese. An enormous dragon is paraded through the streets, accompanied by lights, music, dance, and fireworks.

Enjoy this book with your class:
Lion Dancer: Ernie Wan's Chinese New Year by Kate Waters and Madeline Slovenz Low (Scholastic, 1990).

I hope we all get along.

I wish for good luck.

Let's be friends.

 New Year Clean-Up

Another Chinese custom is to make everything clean and tidy for the New Year. Take this opportunity to involve the children in cleaning and organizing the classroom.

 Good Luck Messages

To make sure that the New Year brings good luck, Chinese children write cheerful messages and good wishes on red paper on New Year's Day.

Steps to follow:
1. Cut strips of red construction paper and ask each child to dictate a cheerful message or good wish for the year. (Ask parent volunteers or students from a fourth or fifth grade class to help with the dictation.)

2. Mount each message on red patterned wrapping paper or shiny red foil.

3. Display on a bulletin board.

Make a Box Dragon

As part of your discussion of Chinese New Year, show children several pictures of dragon parades. Explain that you are going to create a class dragon.

Materials:
- boxes in assorted sizes, at least three or four fairly large
- clothesline-weight rope
- cardboard, posterboard, colored paper
- masking tape
- tempera paint
- crepe paper, tissue paper
- glue
- sequins, feathers, buttons, felt scraps

Teacher preparation:
Arrange several boxes in a row from largest to smallest to form the dragon's head, body, and tail. Punch a hole in the sides of the boxes that are adjacent to each other. Fasten the boxes together with short lengths of rope. Make a knot in the rope on the inside of each box.

Creating the dragon:
Allow the children to paint the dragon. It should be big enough so that everyone can participate. When the paint has dried thoroughly, encourage children to add scales, claws, and decorations made of colored paper, tissue, felt, etc. You may want to divide the class into two groups. One group can paint the dragon; the other group can decorate it.

Extension:
Give your dragon a name and work with the group to develop a group story about the dragon. Chart the story. Carry your dragon through the school in your own "dragon parade."

Martin Luther King, Jr.'s Birthday January 15

Martin Luther King dedicated his life to battling injustice and helping others. He believed in the equality of all people. He thought that change could be brought about without the use of violence. For a beautiful, age-appropriate exploration of Martin Luther King's life and work, read:
Happy Birthday, Martin Luther King by Jean Marzollo (Scholastic, 1993).

★ Conflict Resolution Techniques

Martin Luther King, Jr.'s birthday is the perfect time to introduce some conflict resolution techniques to the children in your classroom. Even very young children can benefit from this kind of activity.

Of course, by this point in the year you will have already established some clear rules about treating others as you want them to treat you. Lead students in a discussion about how to respond to unkind words and actions.

Discuss some possible problems that children may encounter, such as being excluded from play or being hit by another child. Brainstorm together to find appropriate responses that are nonviolent and nonaggressive.

Some options include:
Talk it out.
Listen to one another's viewpoint.
Say how you feel.
Walk away.
Tell a way that you would respond next time.
Reach a compromise.

Remember that although it is your aim to encourage students to develop assertiveness, independence, and self-reliance, always intervene if a child is unable to cope with a situation or is in danger of being hurt.

★ A "King" Circle

This technique for solving interpersonal conflicts bears the name of Martin Luther King, Jr. With frequent use, even young children can become adept at seeing a variety of solutions to problems.

1. When some conflict has arisen, bring children together and seat them in a circle.
2. Ask those involved in the conflict to role play their problem in the center of the circle. Urge them to find a peaceful solution. Allow observing children to make suggestions or demonstrate solutions.

⭐ Conflict Resolution Puppets

Reproduce the puppets on page 8. Color, cut, and glue to tagboard. Attach a tongue depressor or strip of heavy cardboard for a handle.

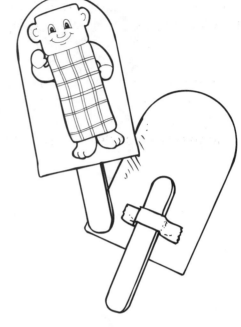

Allow children to take turns using the puppets to act out these sample scenarios. Prompt the child with the first puppet to set up the scene. Encourage the children with the other puppets to respond constructively. Some sample responses are given.

Exclusion/Unwillingness to Share
First puppet:
"You can't play here! I was here first!"

Possible responses:
"Yes I can. The sandbox is for everyone. We can both use it."
"I'd like a turn when you are finished."

Hitting
First puppet:
(pantomimes hitting another puppet)

Possible responses:
"Stop that! That hurt me!"
"Tell me why you hit me. Use your words!"
"I don't hurt anyone and I don't like anyone to hurt me!"

Unkind Remarks
First puppet:
(Use the striped puppet.) "You have polka dots. You're funny looking."

Possible responses:
"I am not. I like my dots and I like me!"
"That hurts my feelings!"
"If you can't say something nice, don't say anything."
"I like your stripes and I like my dots."

If desired, allow each child to create a set of puppets to take home and use with their families to demonstrate their new skills.

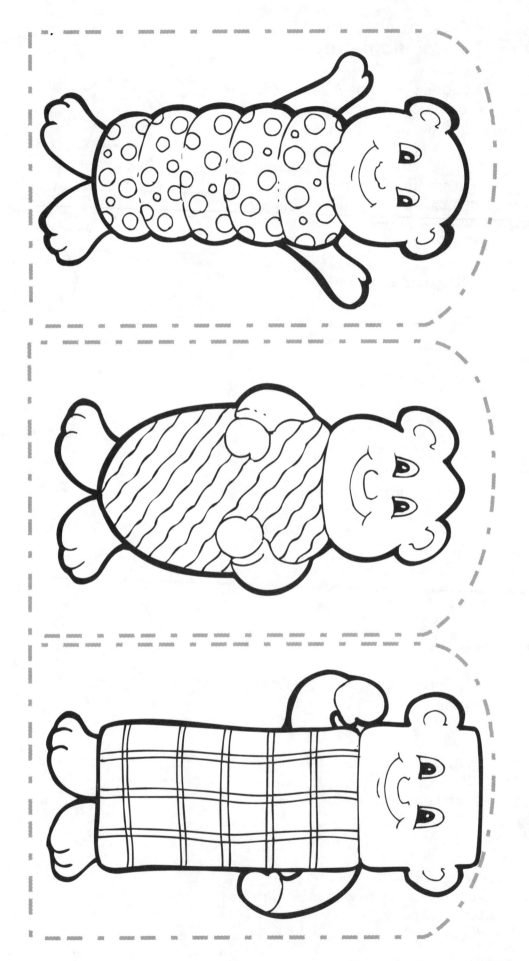

8

Groundhog Day

Groundhog Day is celebrated on February 2. It is a fun holiday built around the superstition that if a groundhog comes out of his hole on this day and sees his shadow, he will be frightened and return to his hole. If this happens, six more weeks of winter weather can be expected. However, if he does not see his shadow, spring weather is on its way.

This observance was brought to America by German farmers who had watched badgers in their homeland to forecast the weather. They adapted the superstition to the groundhog that was common in the woods and fields of their new homes.

The groundhog itself is a chubby member of the squirrel family. It is a type of marmot, sometimes called a woodchuck. It grows to two feet in length, including its bushy tail. The groundhog has thick gray fur with a yellowish-orange belly. Groundhogs build complex burrow systems in the ground for their homes, where they hibernate during the winter.

★ Groundhog Puppet

❶ Reproduce the pattern on page 11 on card stock.

❷ Direct children to color and cut out the groundhog and the tunnel.

❸ Tape the groundhog to a straw.

❹ Roll tunnel and tape or staple.

Take the puppets and tunnels outside. Read the rhyme on page 10, encouraging children to dramatize the actions with their puppets. Have children look for shadows as they "pop" their groundhogs out of the tunnels!

Mr. Groundhog

Out of his tunnel
From the earth below
Up pops Mr. Groundhog!
Ask him what he knows.

Will we have sunshine?
Will there be more snow?
Ask Mr. Groundhog!
Only he will know!

Holiday Fun • EMC 742

1. **Color**
2. **Cut**
3. **Paste**
4. **Pop-up**

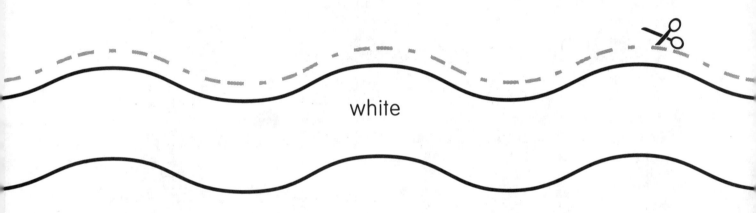

white

brown

Animal Shadows

Materials:
- posterboard
- card stock
- craft sticks
- strong light source (overhead projector or slide projector)

Steps to follow:

❶ Use the patterns to create posterboard templates.

❷ Children trace and cut out animals of their choice on card stock.

❸ Tape sticks on back of animal cutouts for handles.

❹ Set up the projector so that it illuminates a blank wall several feet away. Allow small groups of children to experiment casting shadows with their animal cutouts.

Children will discover that the closer their cutout is to the light source the larger the shadow will be.

Caution children not to look directly at the light source.

Some excellent books on shadows include:
Shadows and Reflections by Tanya Hoban
A Garden for Groundhog by Lorna Balian

For more science information and activities on shadows, see ***Learning About Light and Shadow, EMC 851.***

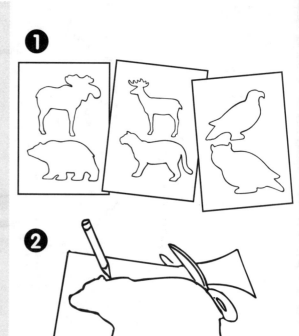

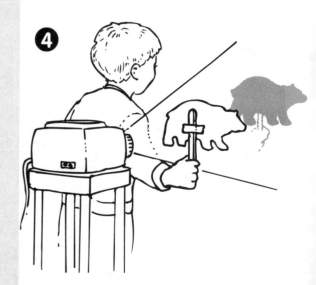

Holiday Fun • EMC 742

Abraham Lincoln's Birthday*   February 12

Abraham Lincoln was the sixteenth president of the United States. He was born in Kentucky in a log cabin on February 12, 1809. Abraham Lincoln was known as a hard worker. He was so renowned for his honesty that he is sometimes referred to as "Honest Abe."

Read your class a book about Abraham Lincoln. Here are two that are colorful and age-appropriate:

Honest Abe by Edith Kunhardt; Greenwillow Books, 1993.
A Picture Book of Abraham Lincoln by David A. Adler; Holiday House, 1989.

★ Lacing Lincoln

This activity provides small motor coordination practice while familiarizing students with the name and image of Abraham Lincoln.

Materials:
- pattern on page 18 reproduced on card stock or heavy paper and cut out
- hole punch
- black yarn or roving
- crayons

Steps to follow:
❶ Use a hole punch to punch out each dot on Lincoln's beard.
❷ Allow children to color the face and hat.
❸ Supply each child with a length of black yarn or roving. Show children how to lace yarn in and out of holes to create beard.
To make lacing easier, wrap one end of the yarn with scotch tape to make a rigid tip.
If children run out of yarn, simply tape the loose end to the back, and continue with a new piece of yarn.

*Note: Abraham Lincoln's and George Washington's birthdays are officially observed on Presidents' Day, the third Monday in February.

17

Lincoln's Log Cabin

Materials:
- pretzel sticks
- 9" x 12" (23 x 30.5 cm) construction paper
- felt or construction paper scraps (optional)
- scissors
- pattern on bottom of this page
- crayons or marking pens
- glue
- pictures of log cabins

Steps to follow:

❶ Show pictures of log cabins and talk about how they were made. Tell children that in Lincoln's time most houses away from cities were built this way.

❷ Reproduce the log cabin for each child.

❸ Children color roof and chimney and cut out cabin.

❹ Glue cabin to construction paper.

❺ Glue pretzels to the front of the cabin to create a log effect.

❻ Plants, animals, and people may be added using felt or paper scraps or crayons and markers.

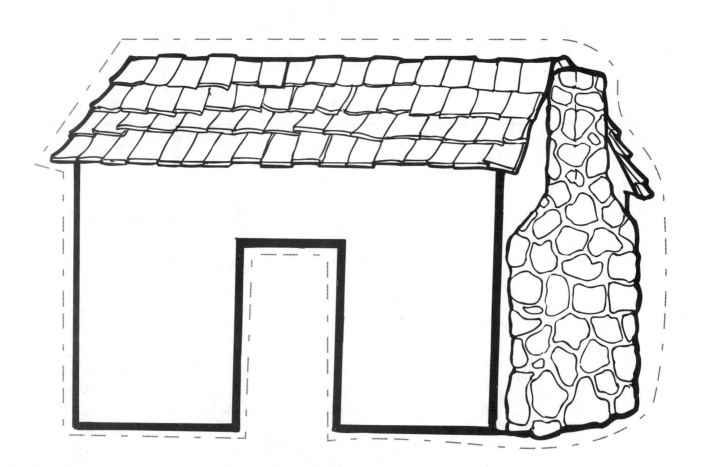

Valentine's Day

Though the origin of Valentine's Day is unclear, we do know that for hundreds of years the day has been associated with love and romance. Today, friends and family members, as well as sweethearts, exchange cards and gifts of candy and flowers.

There are lots of fun ways to celebrate in your classroom. If you choose to have the children exchange valentines, try these tips to make things go smoothly:

- Make valentine bags the day before your party. Set each child's bag at his or her place at the table or in the circle.
- Children must bring enough valentines for everyone in the class. Valentines should not be addressed to individual children. The sender should sign each valentine on the back, but leave the envelope blank.
- Invite children, a few at a time, to "deliver" their valentines. They will file through the room or around the circle, dropping one card into each bag. In this way, delivery of valentines takes only a few minutes.

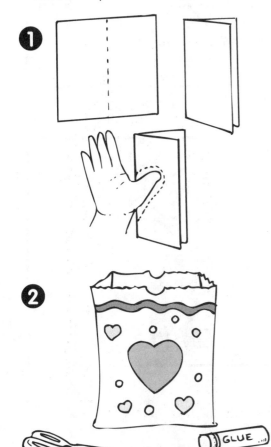

⭐ How to Make a Valentine Bag

Materials:
- white bakery bags (Ask a local bakery for the bags. They will usually give you enough for your class for little or no charge. If you want to be more elaborate, ask for the lovely pink bakery boxes.)
- red, pink, purple, and white markers
- tempera paint
- tissue paper, feathers, felt, stickers, doilies, etc.
- glue, scissors
- scrap paper

Steps to follow:
❶ Conduct a heart cutting lesson with scrap paper before beginning with "good" materials. One simple way for young children to cut hearts is to place a thumb at a slight angle to the fold and cut around it.
❷ Give each child a bag or box. Allow them to decorate as desired, choosing from an array of materials.

These same materials can be used to create valentine cards.

★ A Valentine Zoo

Materials:
- construction paper in valentine colors
- 9" x 12" (23 x 30.5 cm) manilla or drawing paper
- glue
- scissors

Cut out a generous supply of heart shapes in various colors and sizes. Spread them out on the table. Invite children to use hearts to create all kinds of animals. Make scissors and colored paper scraps available so that children may cut out legs, eyes, and so forth, to add to their animals.

★A Valentine Party

Encourage children to wear valentine colors—red, pink, and white—to lend that extra air of festivity to the day's celebrations.

Games
Play this valentine's version of "drop the handkerchief" during your party.

1. Purchase a small length of a valentine design fabric. Cut out a handkerchief-sized square.
2. Have children stand in a circle.
3. Choose one person to be "it." Give this person the handkerchief.
4. "It" skips around the outside of the circle as all sing:

   > A tisket, a tasket,
   > A pretty valentine basket,
   > I wrote a letter to my love
   > And on the way I lost it.

5. "It" drops the handkerchief behind any child. This child picks up the handkerchief and chases "it" around the circle. "It" tries to make it around the circle to take the empty space. If "it" is caught, she/he must be "it" again. If she/he makes it, the chaser becomes "it."

Stories
Read these fun Valentine stories:
The Valentine Cat by Clyde Robert Bulla; Troll, 1987.
Little Mouse's Big Valentine by Thacher Hurd; Troll, 1990.

A Valentine's Day Poem
Reproduce the poem on page 22 for children to color and take home to share with their families. Encourage children to memorize the poem.

Food
Ask parents to contribute heart-shaped foods: cookies, bread cut into heart shapes and spread with cream cheese and raspberry jam, cherry or strawberry finger gelatin cut into heart shapes.

Be sure to save time for children to pass out valentines. Allow them to open and enjoy their valentines as they eat their snacks.

Valentine's Day

Valentine's Day is a time for hearts,
A time for poems and cherry tarts.

Valentine's Day is a time for sweets,
For candy kisses and yummy treats.

Valentine's Day is a time for friends,
A time for love that never ends.

George Washington's Birthday February 22

George Washington was the first president of the United States and is sometimes called the father of our country. He was born in the year 1732.

He was known for his truthfulness and his leadership. One of the most famous stories about George Washington probably has no basis in truth, but remains popular because it illustrates an important aspect of his character:

When George was a little boy, he took an ax and chopped down one of his father's cherry trees. George's father was very angry, and demanded to know who had done this terrible deed. George is supposed to have answered, "Father, I cannot tell a lie. I cut down the cherry tree."

As a result of this story, it has become customary to eat cherry pie on George Washington's birthday. Here is a shortcut recipe for you to enjoy with your class.

★ Shortcut Cherry Pie

- 1 can of cherry pie filling
- 1 tube of refrigerator biscuits
- granulated sugar

Place the cherry pie filling in an 8" x 8" baking pan. Separate refrigerator biscuits. Roll in granulated sugar and arrange on top of pie filling. Bake at 350° for about 20 minutes or until biscuits are golden brown.

This will serve 8–12 children.

While your class is enjoying their cherry pie, read *George Washington, A Picture Biography* by James Cross Giblin; Scholastic, 1992.

⭐ A Portrait of George Washington

This easy-to-make craft project results in a handsome wall hanging.

Explain to children that well-dressed gentlemen of Washington's day wore white powdered wigs and ruffled shirts. If possible, find some pictures to share that illustrate this style of dress.

Materials:
- patterns on page 25 reproduced on white paper
- 6" x 9" (15 x 23 cm) blue construction paper
- cotton balls
- star stickers

Steps to follow:

❶ Color the face a light flesh tone and cut out.

❷ Cut out George Washington's nameplate and ruffles.

❸ Glue face in the center of the blue construction paper.

❹ Glue nameplate at top of the blue construction paper.

❺ Glue the ruffles under the face. Begin with the bottom ruffle, overlapping slightly, as shown.

❻ Glue cotton ball hair to top and sides of face. (Demonstrate how to pull cotton balls apart to make more realistic-looking hair.)

❼ Add star stickers to each corner.

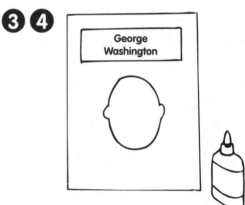

George Washington

Moomba Festival

The Moomba Festival is an eleven-day opportunity for the people of Australia to gather together for fun. Moomba is a word in the language of the native people of Australia, the Aborigines, which means "to join together to have fun."

Moomba is celebrated with parades, sporting events, music and, especially, lots of clowns.

❶

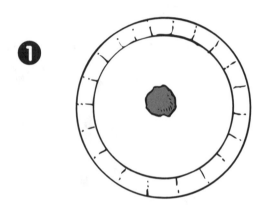

❷

⭐ Clown Faces

Tell the class about the Moomba festival. Show several pictures of clowns and discuss the features observed, pointing out the designs and shapes. Tell the class that they are going to create clown faces of their own.

Materials:
- paper plates
- large red pompons
- felt and fabric scraps
- sequins
- yarn
- construction paper scraps
- scissors
- glue

Steps to follow:
❶ Glue a red pompon in the center of the paper plate for a nose.
❷ Use the other materials to create funny features. You may wish to cut the felt and fabric into small geometric shapes for the children to choose from, as it can be difficult for young children to cut these materials.

Display a parade of clowns along the classroom wall or along a hallway outside your classroom.

　　　　　　　　Holiday Fun • EMC 742

St. Patrick's Day

St. Patrick's Day originated in Ireland, and celebrating it with your class can be a great opportunity to learn a little bit about the "Emerald Isle." One story tells that St. Patrick drove all of the snakes out of Ireland. Make these fun wiggly snakes to commemorate that event.

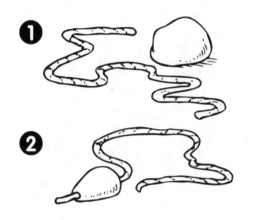

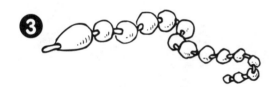

★ Wiggly Snakes

Materials:
- 2' (60 cm) of heavy string or yarn for each student
- tempera paints
- for papier-mâché clay
    - one roll of single-ply toilet tissue
    - water
    - flour
    - large mixing bowl

How to make papier-mâché clay:
1.   Unroll tissue and tear into short lengths.
2.   Place tissue in a large bowl with enough water to thoroughly wet paper. Stir until the paper begins to come apart.
3.   Add flour (and more water if needed) until dough has desired consistency. It should be soft and pliable but not wet.

Steps to follow:
❶ Give each child a length of string and a handful of clay.
❷ Pinch off a small piece of clay and mold it over the end of the string to form the head of the snake. Leave a little bit of the string sticking out for a tongue.
❸ Pinch off another piece of clay and mold it over the string right behind the head. Continue this process, making each piece of clay successively smaller.
❹ Set snakes aside to dry.
❺ Paint with tempera as desired.

⭐ A Saint Patrick's Day Party

Explain to students that green is the color associated with Ireland. Show some pictures of the Irish countryside to illustrate the point. (National Geographic is a good resource.) Tell the class that people wear green on St. Patrick's Day to show that they are thinking about Ireland. Remind students to wear green to school for your St. Patrick's Day festivities.

⭐ Baked Potato Bar

Explain to children that the potato is a favorite and important food in Ireland, and that you are going to eat baked potatoes at your party.

You will need:
- a small baked potato for each person
- small paper plates
- sour cream (low or nonfat for health)
- butter (or low fat margarine)
- chives or chopped green onions
- chopped steamed broccoli
- grated cheddar cheese
- bacon bits

Ask parents to provide the paper goods and toppings. If you do not have access to a large oven at school, bake the potatoes at home. Bring them to school in a large covered roasting pan, wrapped in towels. The potatoes will stay warm for several hours.

When you are ready to eat, set everything out "buffet" style and allow children to help themselves.

While the children are enjoying their potatoes, read ***Jamie O'Rourke and the Big Potato*** by Tomie de Paola (Putnam, 1992).

⭐ Find the Pot of Gold

This is a fun game to play at your St. Patrick's Day party. Set the stage for the game by sharing stories about leprechauns and their gold:

Clever Tom and the Leprechaun by Linda Shute; Scholastic, 1988.
The Hungry Leprechaun by Mary Calhoun; Morrow Junior Books, 1962.

Materials:
- a green top hat, available at party goods stores in March
- a "pot of gold"—a small bean pot or black plastic kettle (look for these around Halloween time) filled with gold-wrapped chocolate coins

How to play:
❶ Have children sit in a circle on the floor.

❷ Place one chair in the center of the circle, and choose a child to be the leprechaun.

❸ The leprechaun will put on the hat and sit on the chair. Place a blindfold over his/her eyes.

❹ Set the pot of gold behind his/her chair.

❺ The children chant:
    Leprechaun, leprechaun
    Funny little man
    Who has your pot of gold?
    Find it if you can.

❻ The teacher silently signals for one child to creep up and steal the pot of gold. The child then returns to her/his place in the circle and sets the pot of gold out of sight behind her/his back.

❼ The blindfold is then removed and the "leprechaun" has three chances to guess who has the gold.

Irish Soda Bread

Try this traditional Irish bread. It is easy to make and children like it.

Ingredients:
- 4 cups flour
- 1 teaspoon salt
- 3 teaspoons baking powder
- 1 teaspoon soda
- 1/4 cup sugar
- 1/4 cup butter
- 1 egg
- 1 3/4 cup buttermilk
- 1/2 cup of currants
- extra butter for eating
- salad oil

Materials:
- 2 mixing bowls
- egg beater
- sifter
- cutting board
- large spoon
- dinner fork
- 2 cake pans
- knife

How to make:
❶ Mix dry ingredients.
   Cut in butter. Set aside.
❷ In a separate bowl, beat egg and mix with buttermilk.
❸ Stir into dry ingredients and add currants.
❹ Turn out on floured bowl and knead briefly.
❺ Divide dough into two equal pieces and shape into smooth round loaves.
❻ Place each loaf into lightly greased round cake pans. Pat dough into pans. Cut a large X across the top of each loaf using a sharp, floured knife. Bake at 375° for 35–40 minutes.
❼ Cut into wedges and serve with butter.

April Fools' Day

It is unclear exactly how our practice of playing jokes on each other on the first day of April originated. The most likely explanation is that it began in France over four hundred years ago. A new calendar was adopted which moved the observance of the New Year from April 1 to January 1. It was hard for people to get used to, and those who continued to celebrate on April 1 were teased and called "April Fools" or "April Fish." Over time, April 1 has become a day for teasing and joking with everyone!

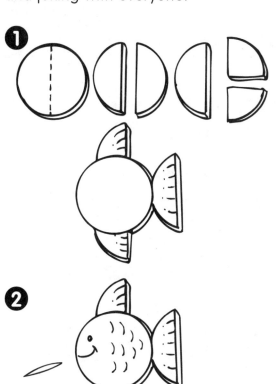

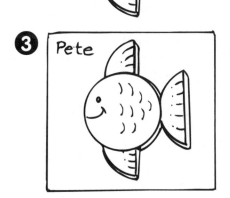

★ Fish Cookies

In France, children receive chocolate fish on April 1. Make these simple fish cookies with your students for a fun April Fools' Day activity.

Materials:
- refrigerated sugar cookie dough (slice and bake)
- small plastic knives
- paper plates
- toothpicks
- cookie sheets
- baking parchment

❶ Give each child two slices of cookie dough on a paper plate. Demonstrate how to cut and arrange the slices to make a fish shape.

❷ Have students press dough together at each seam. Show students how to use a toothpick to add details.

❸ Put each child's name and cookie on a piece of baking parchment. Bake the cookies according to package directions. Eat and enjoy!

     Holiday Fun • EMC 742

Easter

Easter is a very important and joyful Christian holiday that celebrates the resurrection of Christ. Many of the customs that are associated with Easter, however, have pagan roots and have been incorporated into the popular secular observance of the holiday. Bunnies, eggs, flowers and a celebration of spring and new life are symbols of this happy time of year.

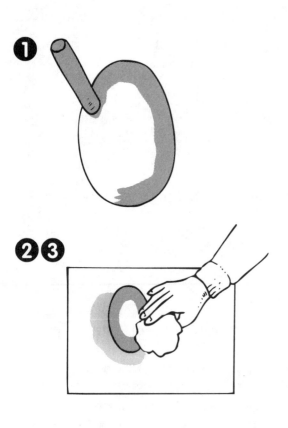

★ Chalk Outlines

Materials:
• white or pastel-colored construction paper
• colored chalk
• templates on pages 33 & 34
• facial tissues

Teacher preparation:
Copy the patterns onto light cardboard. Cut out to form templates. Make enough so that children who will be participating in the activity at any one time will have several choices of templates.

Steps to follow:
Be sure to model these steps for children.

❶ Rub a heavy layer of colored chalk around the outer edge of a template.

❷ Hold the template down carefully on a sheet of construction paper.

❸ Use a tissue to wipe the chalk from the center of the template, over the edge, and onto the paper.

Many templates and colors can be used and overlapped to create a lively spring design.

       Holiday Fun • EMC 742

Holiday Fun • EMC 742

★ Sponge-Painted Eggs

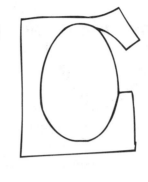

Materials:
- 9" x 12" (23 x 30.5 cm) pastel-colored construction paper
- sea sponges
- tempera paint
- pie pans
- clothespins

Teacher preparation:

❶ Cut out large egg shapes from pastel-colored construction paper.

❷ Tear sponges into approximately 2" x 2" (5 x 5 cm) pieces.

❸ Clip one piece of sponge into each clothespin.

❹ Pour a very thin layer of tempera into pie pans. Place several sponges in each color.

❺ Ready a bulletin board to display finished eggs.

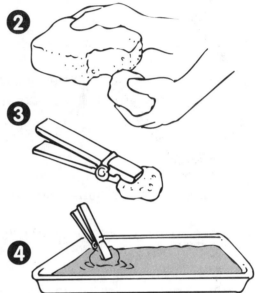

Steps to follow:

1. Explain to children that it is very important to avoid mixing the colors.

2. Demonstrate how to hold the clothespin without squeezing, dip the sponge lightly in the paint, and dab it onto the paper egg.

3. Color can be applied in stripes, spots, or at random.

4. After the eggs dry, use them to decorate a bulletin board.

Bunny Bread

Make bunny bread to take home as a seasonal gift.

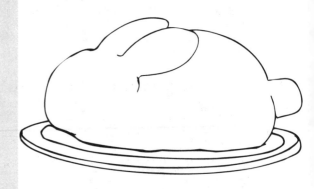

Materials for each student:
- one-half stick of frozen bread dough, thawed
- a square of aluminum foil
- butter
- 1 marshmallow
- 1 toothpick

Ask parents to provide materials. (You will need one package of frozen bread dough for each group of 4 students.)

Steps to follow:
Demonstrate steps 3–6 before students begin. Enlist parent help to supervise small groups.

❶ Make sure students wash hands before any cooking activity.

❷ Have each child rub a tiny bit of butter on both hands to prevent the dough from sticking.

❸ Give each student a piece of foil and 1/2 stick of bread dough.

❹ Pinch the dough in half. Roll one half of the dough into an oval shape and place on the foil.

5 Pinch the remaining dough in half again. Roll one half into a ball. Join the ball to the end of the oval to form the head, pinching it together firmly.

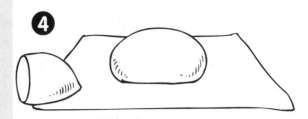

6 Roll the remaining dough into two little logs. Pinch these onto the head to form ears.

Bake according to package directions, decreasing time to adjust for the smaller size loaves.

7 When loaves are completely cooled, attach a marshmallow tail to each with a toothpick.

★ Bird's Nests

It is best to work with small groups of children when doing this activity.

(One recipe makes about 12 nests)
Ingredients:
- 6 large shredded wheat biscuits
- 10-ounce package marshmallows
- 3 tablespoons margarine
- salad oil for hands
- jelly beans or candy eggs

Materials:
- large bowl
- saucepan
- hot plate
- spoon
- waxed paper

Steps to follow:

❶ Allow children to break up shredded wheat biscuits in large bowl. Set aside.

❷ In saucepan on a hot plate, melt margarine and marshmallows together. Stir to blend.

❸ Remove from heat and pour in shredded wheat. Quickly stir until all cereal is coated.

❹ Place a spoonful of mixture on a sheet of waxed paper for each child.

❺ When mixture is cool enough to be safe, but still soft, have children grease their hands and shape a bird's nest.

❻ Provide jelly beans, or other candy eggs for each nest.

❼ Eat for a fun snack, or take home as a decoration.

★ A Bunny Finger Play

When you introduce this finger play, you can use the five fingers of one hand to represent the bunnies or make finger puppets using the patterns below. Pantomime the actions in each line.

Five little bunnies, hopping down the lane
The first one said, "I think it's going to rain."
The second one said, "It will make the flowers bloom."
The third one said, "I can hear the thunder boom!"
The fourth one said, "I feel a drop."
The fifth one said, "Come on! Let's hop!"
Then the lightning flashed and the rain poured down
And the bunnies hopped fast to their home in the ground.

Each time the rhyme is repeated, let a new child use the finger puppets.

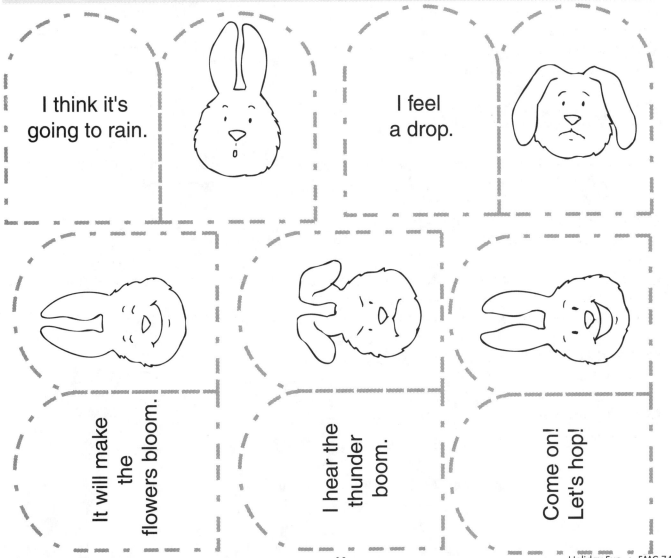

I think it's going to rain.

I feel a drop.

It will make the flowers bloom.

I hear the thunder boom.

Come on! Let's hop!

Arbor Day

Arbor Day is a day that has been set aside to acknowledge the importance of trees. Many individuals and groups in the United States and Canada plant trees on Arbor Day.

Trees benefit us in many ways. They provide us with beauty and shade, with wood to make many products, and they help to clean and improve the air by taking in carbon dioxide and giving off oxygen. Trees are essential to the well being of our planet and the people who live on it.

Early in the year, ask children to bring in a variety of seeds from fruits such as apples, pears, oranges, etc. Plant the seeds in paper cups and label them. Keep them watered and watch for sprouting. Put at least 2 seeds in each cup and plant extra cups since, inevitably, some will fail to sprout.

★ Arbor Day Ceremony

On April 22, have an Arbor Day ceremony in your class. Give each child a new tree to take home and plant. Use this choral reading with its easy-to-learn response line as part of your Arbor Day ceremony.

Speaker 1: We celebrate Arbor Day because
All: We love trees.
Speaker 2: Trees help to clean the air.
All: We love trees.
Speaker 3: Trees give us cooling shade.
All: We love trees.
Speaker 4: Trees give us fruits to eat.
All: We love trees.
Speaker 5: Trees give us paper and wood.
All: We love trees.
Speaker 6: Trees are homes for animals and birds.
All: We love trees.
Speaker 7: We celebrate Arbor Day because
All: We love trees.

★ Leaf Rubbings

Materials:
- large, well-veined leaves
- unwrapped crayons—red, orange, purple, yellow
- newsprint
- scissors

Steps to follow:
1. Place a leaf on the table, vein side up.
2. Put a sheet of newsprint over the leaf.
3. Rub the side of a crayon across the paper several times, creating an outline of the leaf.
4. Move the newsprint and create a rubbed leaf in a new place on the paper. Continue until the design is to your liking.
5. Mount the designs on a bulletin board backed with black paper.

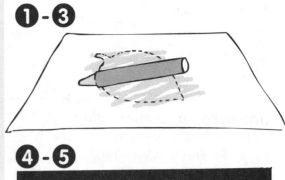

★ Leaf Prints

Materials:
- large, well-veined leaves
- tempera paints
- newsprint
- scissors
- newspapers

Steps to follow:
1. Cover a table with newspapers.
2. Place a leaf on the table, vein side up.
3. Paint the vein side of the leaf with a light coating of tempera.
4. Press a sheet of newsprint on top of the painted leaf.
5. Lift the paper off carefully. Set aside to dry.
6. When the print is dry, cut around the edge with a pair of scissors.

This technique creates lifelike prints. Use them to: border bulletin boards, staple to a paper plate ring to form a wreath, hang on strings to create a leaf mobile.

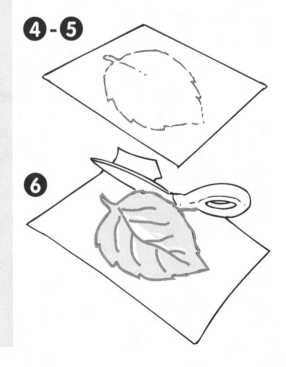

★ Johnny Appleseed

John Chapman, better known as Johnny Appleseed, devoted much of his life to planting trees and creating orchards in the frontier settlements of early America. No one really knows if the many folk tales about Johnny Appleseed are true, but he did plant hundreds of acres in orchards and is remembered as a friend of the trees.

Read a story about Johnny Appleseed:
Johnny Appleseed Goes a 'Planting by Patsy Jensen; Troll, 1994.
Johnny Appleseed, A Tall Tale retold by Steven Kellogg; Scholastic, 1989.

Follow-up learning about Johnny Appleseed with this art project.

★ Apple Prints

Materials:
- apples, cut in half
- white or tan construction paper—9" x 12" (23 x 30.5 cm)
- green, red, and yellow tempera paints
- paper plates
- markers

Steps to follow:
❶ Spread each color of tempera paint into a very thin layer on a separate paper plate.
❷ Place several apple halves by each color. (Hint: Remind children not to dip an apple into more than one color.)
❸ Dip the cut side of the apple into the paint and stamp it onto the paper. Repeat, using other colors.
❹ When prints are dry, use markers to add seeds, leaves, and stems.

Holiday Fun • EMC 742

May Day

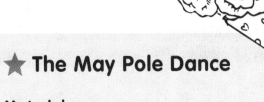

Long ago in England, the coming of spring was celebrated on May Day. People would go into the woods and fields to cut flowers and greenery to freshen and beautify their homes. Today's May Day festivities still center around flowers and spring.

★ The May Pole Dance

Materials:
- a crepe paper streamer for each student
- strong tape

Tape one end of each streamer to a tetherball pole, basketball net post, or tree without low branches.

Children dance around the May Pole winding their streamers around it as they go. If you have a large group of children, create an inner and an outer ring. Have one ring move clockwise while the other moves counterclockwise. Reverse the order of movement to unwind the pole.

The children may enjoy repeating this process several times as you play some appropriate music. Try "Spring" from Vivaldi's **Four Seasons**.

★ May Pole Dance Costumes

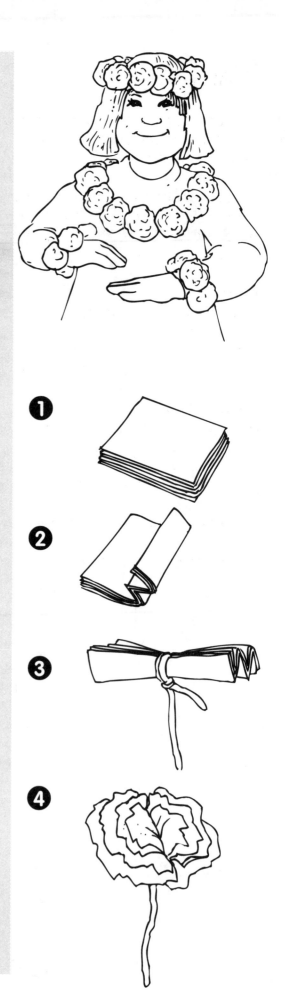

Help children decorate themselves for the May Pole Dance. Make tissue paper flowers and use them to create necklaces, bracelets, and crowns using the directions that follow.

Materials:
- 6" (15 cm) squares of tissue paper
- real flowers (optional)
- 1" (2.5 cm) elastic
- chenille stems and twist ties
- blunt embroidery needles and embroidery floss
- sentence strips
- stapler
- glue

Tissue Flowers
❶ Stack 6 squares of tissue paper.
❷ Fold the stack of squares back and forth, fan style.
❸ Twist a chenille stem tightly around the center. If no stem is wanted on the flower, use a twist tie in place of the chenille stem.
❹ Separate each layer and bunch toward the center.

Use Flowers to Make:
•Flower Necklaces
Create necklaces by threading real or paper flowers onto the embroidery floss using the blunt needle. Make the necklace long enough to fit easily over child's head. Tie ends.

•Flower Bracelets
Measure a length of elastic that fits comfortably around the wrist and ankle. Add a few inches and tie the ends together snugly. Glue a paper flower onto the elastic. Let dry and then slide onto wrist or ankle.

•Flower Crowns
Cut a sentence strip to fit around child's head. Staple into circle. Glue on paper flowers to create a flower crown.

★ May Cone

A sweet May Day tradition is to fill a paper cone with flowers and leave it on the doorstep of a friend or neighbor.

Make the cone below and fill it with real or paper flowers. Remind children to be sure that a parent accompanies them when they make their secret May Day deliveries.

Materials:
- lightweight paper plates
- markers, crayons
- stapler
- real or paper flowers (see page 44)

Steps to follow:

❶ Cut plates in half, giving each student one half of a plate.

❷ Allow students to color plates as desired.

❸ Fold plate into cone shape and staple.

❹ Fill with flowers and deliver.

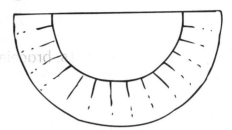

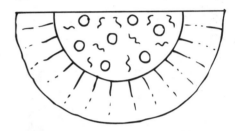

Holiday Fun • EMC 742

Cinco de Mayo

Cinco de Mayo, the fifth of May, is a holiday in Mexico. Cinco de Mayo commemorates Mexico's victory over France in the Battle of Puebla in 1862. Though it is not one of Mexico's most important holidays, it is familiar to many Americans as it is celebrated in hispanic communities throughout the U.S. Celebrate Cinco de Mayo in your classroom with a little bit of Mexico's marvelous food and music.

★ Make Quesadillas

Quesadillas are easy to make and are sure to be a hit with your students.

Ingredients:
- large flour tortillas
- grated Monterey Jack cheese

Steps to follow:
1. Place a tortilla in a dry electric skillet. Use no oil.
2. Heat quickly on both sides.
3. Place a handful of grated cheese on half of the tortilla, folding the other half over.
4. Continue to heat until the cheese is melted.
5. Remove to a plate and cut in wedges.
6. Serve plain or with mild salsa or guacamole.

The quesadillas will be even better if the children make their own tortillas.

Ingredients:
- 8 cups flour
- 1 cup solid vegetable shortening
- 4 teaspoons salt
- 2 cups lukewarm water
- butter

Steps to follow:
1. Mix flour, shortening, and salt together with hands until well blended.
2. Stir in water.
3. Knead until smooth.
4. Divide dough into 24 balls. Give each child a ball of dough to pat and stretch into an 8- or 9-inch circle.
5. Cook both sides of tortillas on an ungreased griddle, until dry and speckled brown.
6. Serve with butter, or use to make quesadillas.

★ Make Maracas

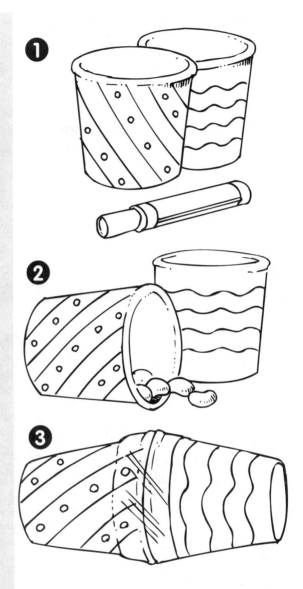

Make these maracas and play along with some mariachi music. Point out to children that different fillings make quite a difference in the sound of the maracas!

Materials:

- 2 styrofoam cups for each child
- clear packing tape at least 2" (5 cm) wide
- various fillings - dried kidney beans, garbanzo beans, rice, etc.

Steps to follow:

❶ Allow children to decorate outside of cups with brightly colored markers.

❷ Place a few dried beans or a handful of rice in one cup.

❸ Place the other cup on top, upside down. Join cups together with a strip of the packing tape. Be sure to use packing tape so that maracas will not come apart!

Mother's Day

2nd Sunday in May

Mother's Day became a nationally recognized holiday in the United States in 1914. This came about largely through the efforts of a woman named Anna Jarvis, who wanted to do something to pay special tribute to her own mother—and to all mothers.

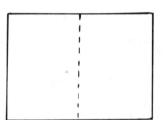

★ Mother's Day Card

This is a Mother's Day card that is sure to be treasured forever. Before starting the project, show children a finished sample and prompt them to begin thinking of the memory they will want written in the card.

Materials:
- patterns on page 49
- 9" x 12" (23 x 30.5 cm) construction paper in pastel colors
- crayons or markers
- scissors
- glue

Steps to follow:
1. Allow each child to choose a sheet of construction paper.
   Demonstrate how to fold it to create a card.
2. Cut out the patterns.
3. Glue "I remember when I was little..." to the front of the card. Monitor carefully so that cards don't end up opening backwards.
4. Glue "I am still your baby" on the right inside page of the card. Children draw themselves in the frame.
5. On the left inside page of the card, ask each child to dictate a favorite memory from when they were very small. While you are writing the dictated memories, children can be decorating their cards.

©1998 by Evan-Moor Corp.

Holiday Fun • EMC 742

I remember
when I was little...

I am still your baby!
Love,

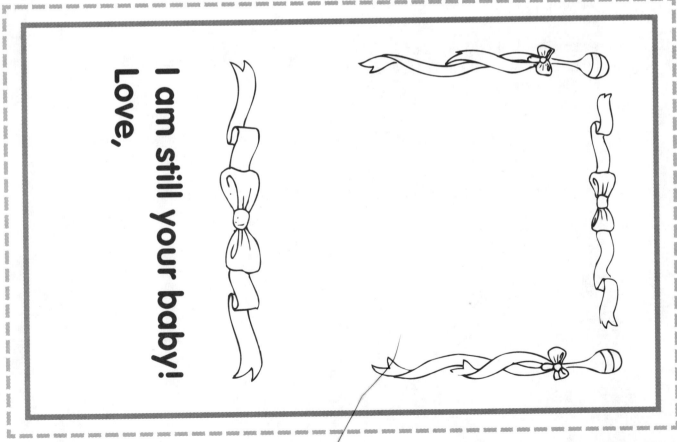

49

Trail Mix for Mom

Moms will be delighted when their children ask them to go for a special Mother's Day hike around the block, in the park, or even in the backyard to share a happy time and the trail mix they've made in class.

Materials:
- small jars with lids or small zipper-lock bags
- Ask parents to contribute 8–12 ounces of any of the following ingredients:
  -shelled nuts: peanuts, almonds, cashews, macadamias, walnuts, pecans
  -chopped dried fruit: raisins, cherries, cranberries, apples, pineapple, papaya, apricots
  -small candy-coated chocolate or peanut butter pieces

Mix all contributions in a large bowl. Scoop out portions for each child to fill a jar or bag.

Option:
If you use small jars, make them look extra special by adding a cloth top.

Cut squares or circles of brightly colored fabric about an inch larger than the jar lids. Glue fabric on the top of the lid. When dry, put lid on jar and tie tightly with narrow ribbon.

★ Coffee Filter Flowers

Make a bouquet of colorful flowers for Mom to enjoy on her day and for many days to come!

Materials:
- white coffee filters (basket type)
- food coloring
- eye droppers
- small jars
- water
- newspapers
- green tissue paper
- green chenille stems

Steps to follow:

❶ Fill jars with water. Squeeze in enough food coloring to give water a dark, rich color.

❷ Put an eyedropper in each jar.

❸ Spread a thick layer of newspaper on a table.

❹ Children use eye droppers to drip colored water on the coffee filters. Remind children not to soak the filters but to use only a few drops of color on each one. It helps if they know that they will be allowed to make as many as they like.

❺ When dry, place the filter on top of a square of green tissue paper. Gather the center of the filter with the tissue on the outside. Twist on a chenille stem to complete the flower.

Memorial Day

Memorial Day is a day set aside to honor and remember all of those brave individuals who have given their lives to keep our country free. Discuss freedom with your class, and lead them in a directed drawing of the Statue of Liberty, a famous symbol of the freedom we cherish.

Kamehameha Day June 11

Many years ago, long before Hawaii became part of the United States, the Hawaiian Islands were ruled by many kings. One of kings, Kamehameha, is remembered because he brought all of the islands together as one kingdom. In Hawaii, Kamehameha Day is celebrated with singing, feasting, and parades.

Bring Kamehameha Day into your classroom with leis (flower garlands) and special helmets like the one worn by King Kamehameha. Add a feast of Hawaiian-inspired foods—a luau—and make it a fun farewell party for your class as school comes to a close for the summer.

❶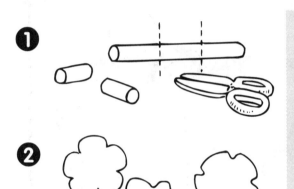

❷

❸

❹

❺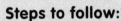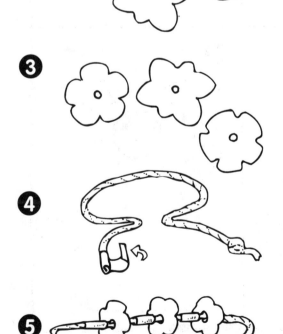

★ Leis

Materials:
- drinking straws (the largest diameter you can find)
- flower patterns on page 54 reproduced on several colors of construction paper
- a 3′ (1 meter) length of yarn for each student
- cellophane tape
- hole punch

Steps to follow:

❶ Cut drinking straws into 1″ segments.

❷ Cut a variety of construction paper flowers. Each student will need about 18 flowers.

❸ Punch holes in the centers of the flowers.

❹ Wrap tape tightly around one end of the yarn to form a "needle." Knot the other end.

❺ Create leis by alternating paper flowers and straw segments.

 Holiday Fun • EMC 742

Holiday Fun • EMC 742

⭐ A Simple Luau

The traditional Hawaiian luau features a whole roasted pig! Enlist parent help to provide ham or turkey-ham slices instead, along with the following goodies:

- Fresh pineapple cut into chunks or slices. (Bring in a whole fresh pineapple for the children to examine.)
- Fresh coconut chunks, removed from the shell. (Bring in a whole fresh coconut for the children to examine.)
- Sugar cane cut into strips for the children to taste. (This can be found in the produce section of some supermarkets or specialty stores.)

⭐ King Kamehameha's Helmet

King Kamehameha wore a beautiful golden helmet with an intriguing shape. Help each child in your class make one for the celebration.

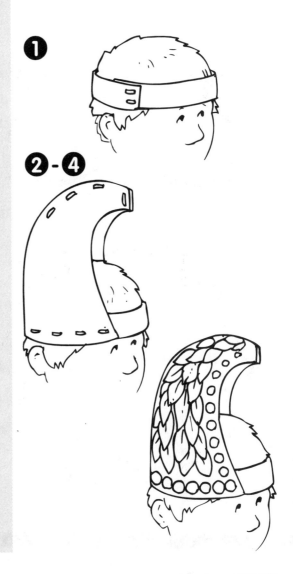

Materials:
- sentence strips
- pattern on page 56 reproduced on 9" x 12" (23 x 30.5 cm) yellow construction paper (2 per student)
- yellow feathers or feather shapes cut from construction paper
- scissors
- sequins
- glue
- stapler

Steps to follow:
❶ Make a base for the helmet. Measure a sentence strip to fit each child's head. Staple.
❷ Cut out the 2 helmet sections.
❸ Staple the bottom edge of the helmet pieces to the sentence strip on each side of the head.
❹ Bring the tops of the helmet pieces together and staple.
❺ Allow children to decorate the helmets with yellow feathers and sequins.

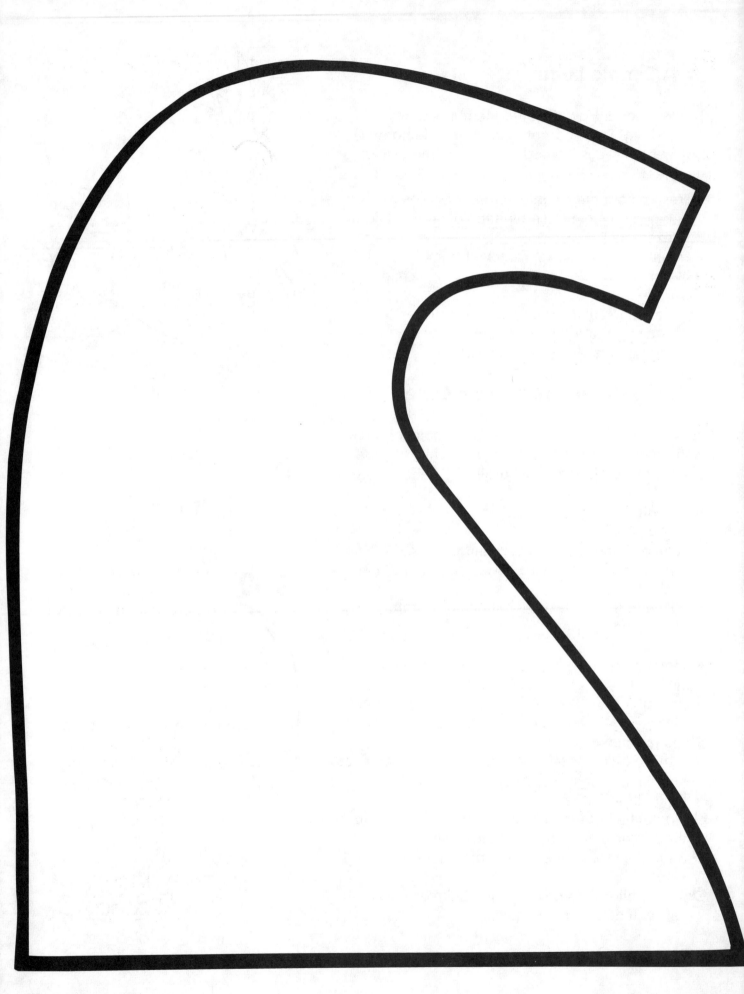

Holiday Fun • EMC 742

Father's Day

For almost a hundred years, the third Sunday in June has been set aside to honor fathers.

★ Leather-Look Pencil Holder and Picture Frame

This is a messy project! Cover tables with newspapers and provide smocks and disposable gloves for children. Work with a small group at a time to provide close supervision.

Materials:
- 5" x 7" (13 x 18 cm) cardboard
- soup can
- felt
- masking tape
- brown paste shoe polish
- glue
- rags
- adhesive picture hangers
- a photograph of each child wearing a cowboy hat and bandanna. Provide hat and bandanna and ask a parent to come in and take pictures of the children.
- optional—western motif metal decorations and/or leather scraps, available at craft stores

Steps to follow:
1. Help children cover soup can with strips of masking tape. Make sure that strips overlap so that whole can is covered. Cover cardboard with tape strips in the same way.
2. With a small rag, apply shoe polish to taped surfaces, producing a tanned leather look. Allow to dry.
3. Glue photo in center of frame.
4. Cut a circle of felt to fit bottom of can and glue on. Glue on metal motifs and leather scraps as desired. Add a picture hanger to the back of the frame.

★ A Special Key Chain

Key chains make wonderful gifts for dads and moms. The chains and the leather fobs are available in craft stores and through Tandy Leather. Call 1-800-555-3130 for the store nearest you or to request a catalog.

The fobs may be tooled using authentic leather tools or simple toolbox items, such as plain and phillips head screwdrivers, nuts and bolts, or any object with a relatively blunt point.

Steps to follow:
❶ Wet the leather fobs.

❷ Stamp the design using various tools and a small hammer.

❸ Punch a hole through the leather for the chain.

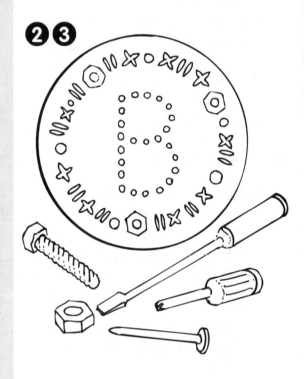

⭐ Number One Dad Pop-Up Card

Unless your children have experience making pop-up cards, this project should be done in groups of no more than four students with an adult or capable fourth grader-or-older to help.

Materials:
- pop-up pattern on page 60
- decoration patterns on page 61
- 6" x 9" (15 x 23 cm) blue construction paper
- glue
- scissors

Steps to follow:

❶ Color and cut out the patterns on page 61. Set aside.

❷ Make the inner card as shown:
- fold the pattern and cut on the lines
- fold and crease the cut strip in both directions
- Open up the paper and push the strip to the inside, reversing and creasing the fold

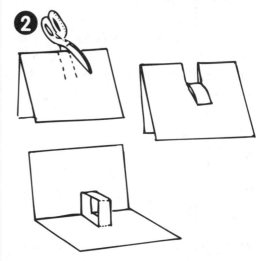

❸ Glue the pop-up into the outer card:
- fold blue paper in half
- close pop-up pattern and place inside blue paper, matching folds
- put glue on top side of pop-up
- close outer card and press
- flip card over and open back
- spread glue on top surface of pop-up
- close card and press

❹ Glue the star to the pop-up tab. Sign the card.

❺ Glue compass and message to the front of card.

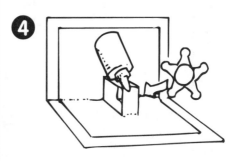

North or South
East or West

My dad is the
very best!

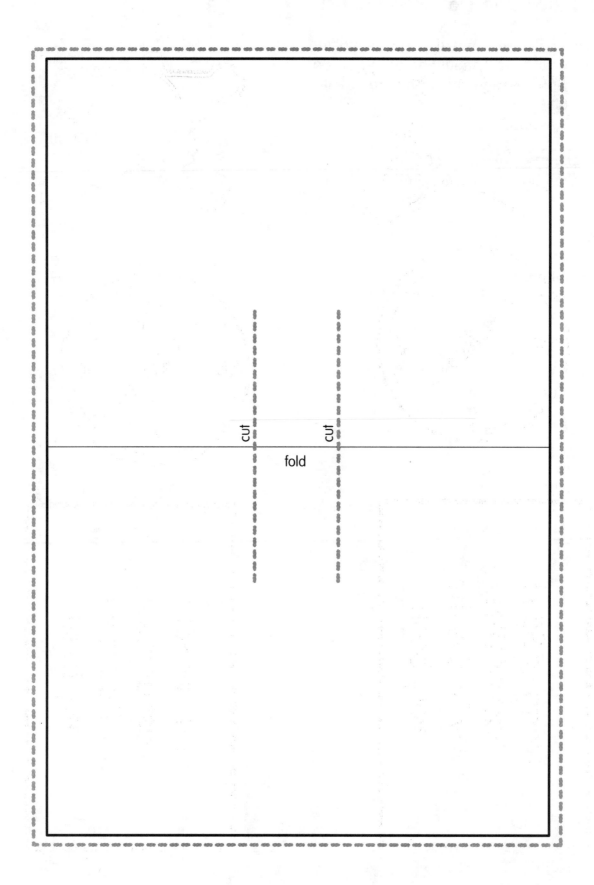

cut

cut

fold

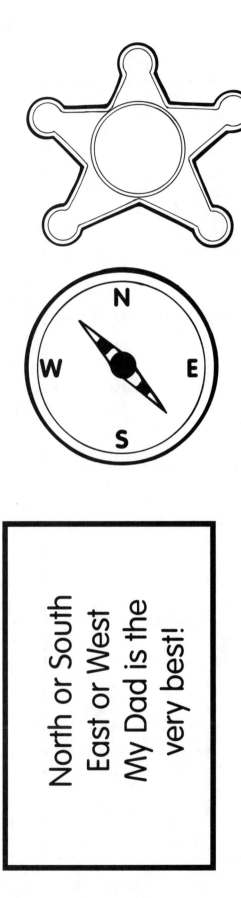

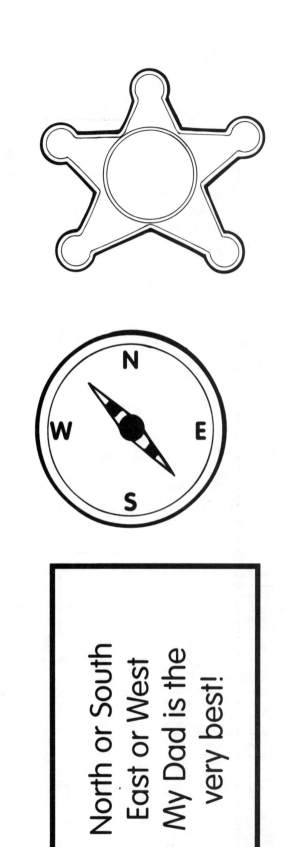

North or South
East or West
My Dad is the
very best!

North or South
East or West
My Dad is the
very best!

Flag Day

Flag Day was first observed in 1877, on the 100th anniversary of the U.S. flag. When the first U.S. flag was created in 1777, the Continental Congress decided that it would have 13 stripes and 13 stars, representing the thirteen states of the union. A new stripe and star were added for each new state. It soon became apparent that adding so many stripes would be impractical. So in 1818, it was decided that the U.S. flag would keep the original thirteen stripes and add a star for each new state.

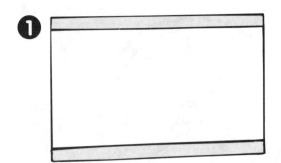

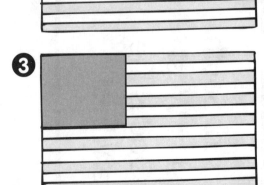

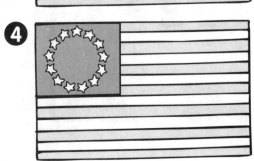

Make original flags to celebrate Flag Day.

Materials:
(for each flag)
• 12" x 18" (30.5 x 45.5 cm) white construction paper
• 1" x 18" (2.5 x 45.5 cm) red construction paper strips
• 7" (18 cm) square of blue construction paper
• 13 star stickers or paper stars punched with star-shaped hole punch

Steps to follow:

❶ Glue a red stripe along the top and bottom of the paper.

❷ Place the five remaining red strips evenly and glue.

❸ Glue blue square in upper left-hand corner of flag.

❹ Arrange 13 stars in a circle on the blue square.

Independence Day

Celebrate America's birthday! On July 4, 1776 America declared its independence from England and began its adventure as a new country. Families in rural communities and big cities alike celebrate Independence Day with picnics, parades, and fireworks.

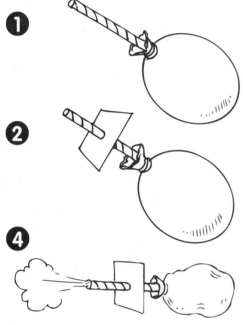

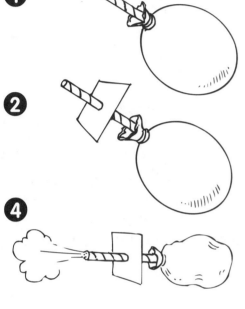

★ Balloon Rockets

These safe "fireworks" are lots of fun, indoors or out.

Materials:
- red, white, and blue balloons
- plastic drinking straws, cut in half
- rubber bands
- small index cards, cut in half

Steps to follow:

❶ Insert straw into balloon opening. Secure with rubber band.

❷ Punch a hole in center of index card. Slide onto straw. This serves as a stabilizer.

❸ Blow up balloon, pinching straw to prevent air from leaking out.

❹ When ready, let go of straw and watch the rocket zoom!

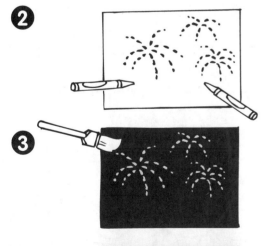

★ Fireworks on Paper

Materials:
- white construction paper
- glitter crayons
- black watercolor paint
- sequins
- glue

Steps to follow:

❶ Show children pictures of fireworks. Discuss fireworks displays they may have seen.

❷ Use glitter crayons to create fireworks "bursts" on paper. Remind them to make dark, heavy marks.

❸ Paint a black watercolor wash over the entire page. Crayon marks will resist the wash and look like fireworks exploding in the night sky.

❹ When the papers are dry, glue a few scattered sequins across the page as an added touch.

★ Eagle Drawing

Discuss the fact that the bald eagle is one symbol of the United States. Bring in items to view that use the eagle as part of the design (back of the dollar bill, the quarter, the presidential seal).

Demonstrate the following steps on the chalkboard or overhead projector. Children will enjoy the feeling of success as they follow the sequence given to create a majestic eagle.

Moon Day

On July 20, 1969 Neil Armstrong, an American astronaut, became the first man to walk on the moon. He said, "One small step for man, one giant leap for mankind" as he stepped onto the moon.

Children love stories about space and space travel. Let each of your students become an astronaut for a day with this easy-to-make "space helmet."

★ Paper Bag Helmet

Materials:
- white paper bags large enough to fit over a child's head (You can find these at your local bakery.)
- laminating film cut into 5" x 7" (13 x 18 cm) pieces
- tape
- scissors
- crayons or markers
- patterns for mask and ear pieces on page 66

Steps to follow:
❶ Color and cut out mask and ear pieces.

❷ Glue to bag as shown.

❸ Assist children in cutting out window area from mask.

❹ Tape a laminating film to the inside of the bag, covering the window area of the mask.

These records have fun selections for dramatizing a space adventure:
On the Move with Greg and Steve, Youngheart Records.
Witches' Brew by Hap Palmer, Activity Records.

Cut out this section.

Labor Day

First Monday in September

This holiday, begun in 1894, honors the American worker. Many communities sponsor parades and families gather to enjoy picnics. Labor Day is considered by many to mark the end of summer and quite often coincides with the beginning of the new school year.

Discuss with the children in your class how these and other people in our community add to the quality of our lives:

police
fire fighters
doctors, nurses, and other health workers
grocers
telephone repairers
clergy
teachers
farmers
bankers
construction workers
cooks
printers
artists
musicians
truck drivers
pilots

Be sure to relate the discussion to the jobs of people in the children's families.

Work together to create a class thank you letter to be sent to some of the people whose hard work makes our lives so good!

Invite the parents or other family members of your students to come and talk to the children about the jobs they do. Ask them to bring in some of the tools they use to do their jobs.

Holiday Fun • EMC 742

Oktoberfest

This German festival began in 1810 to celebrate the wedding of a king and queen. It has been an occasion for merriment ever since. Bring Bavaria into your classroom for this fun fall festival.

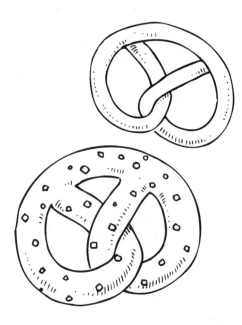

★ Food Treats

1. Ask parents to provide a selection of cheeses and sausages for tasting.

2. Purchase soft pretzels or make your own. It's easy with frozen bread dough.
   - Give each student an egg-sized piece of thawed dough on a sheet of waxed paper.
   - Demonstrate how to roll dough out into a long "snake."
   - Demonstrate how to fold into traditional pretzel shape.
   - Transfer to baking sheets.
   - Brush with lightly beaten egg white and sprinkle with kosher salt.
   - Bake at 350° until golden brown.
   - Serve with mustard.

★ Entertainment

1. Find a recording of polka music to share with the children.

2. Read some of Grimm's fairy tales. A few favorites include:

   Little Red Riding Hood
   Hansel and Gretel
   Cinderella
   Snow White
   Sleeping Beauty
   Rumpelstiltskin

⭐ Jumping Jack

Children will enjoy making this paper puppet that dances. Adult supervision will be necessary for stringing the pieces.

Materials:
- pattern on page 70, reproduced on lightweight tag or card stock
- paper fasteners
- tape
- 24" (61 cm) piece of string
- hole punch
- wooden bead

Steps to follow:
❶ Color each part of the jumping jack and cut out.

❷ Punch holes in the pieces at circles.

❸ Fasten the arms and legs to the body using the second holes from the top. Fasteners need to be a bit loose to allow for movement.

❹ String thread through holes as shown.

❺ Knot the two sections of string between the legs.

❻ Tie the wooden bead to the ends of the string and pull.

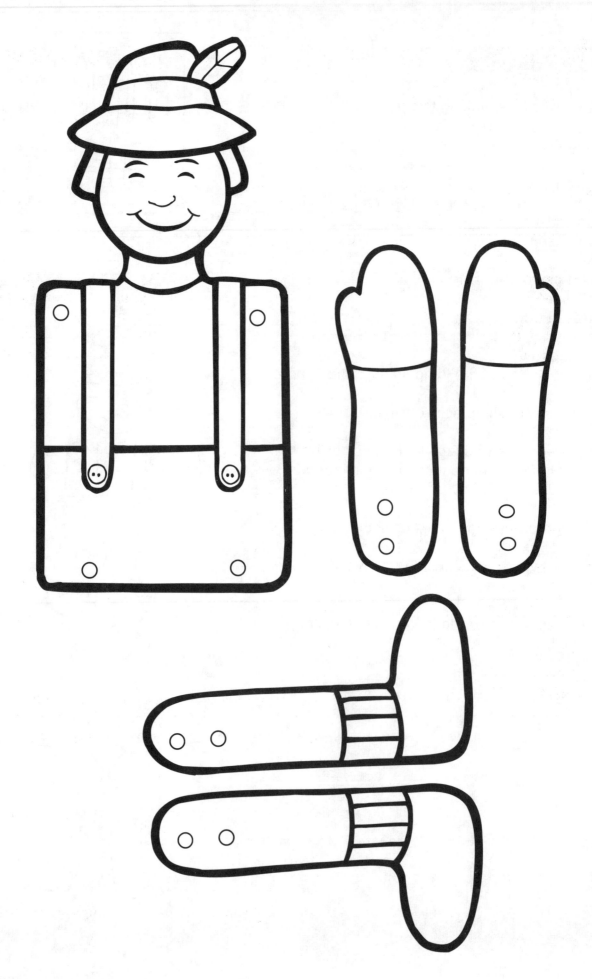

Holiday Fun • EMC 742

Native American Day

This holiday is observed in many U.S. states. It is a day set aside to honor Native American people. Pages 71–81 contain eight different projects from which to choose in celebrating this holiday.

★ Sand Painting

The Pueblo Indians are credited with originating sand painting, although the Navajo people expanded the art form. Sand paintings are made on the floor of a hogan by a priest, for ceremonial purposes. The colored sand is made by grinding various types and colors of rock. Children will enjoy making their own sand paintings using colored grits to fill in the outlines of patterns provided.

Ingredients for colored grits:
- 2 cups of grits for every color
- rubbing alcohol
- food colorings
- zipper-lock plastic bags

How to color grits:
❶ Place 2 cups of uncooked grits in large plastic zipper-lock bag.
❷ Add 2-3 tablespoons of rubbing alcohol and 5–15 drops of food coloring.
❸ Zip bag and shake until color is even.
❹ Spread out on newspaper to dry.
❺ Make a variety of colors and store each in a separate bag. Some "authentic" colors include: dark brown or black, turquoise, orange, and yellow.

Materials for paintings:
- patterns on page 73 and 74 reproduced on tan construction paper or lightweight tagboard
- newspaper
- bowls
- white glue diluted with water
- paper cafeteria tray or aluminum baking tray large enough to hold pattern
- paintbrushes

Steps to follow:

❶ Place pattern on tray. This is your working area.

❷ Paint glue onto small area of pattern.

❸ Carefully take a pinch of the colored grits and sprinkle them on the wet glue to cover.

❹ Shake excess grits into tray and return them to the bowl of the same color.

❺ Continue working in this manner, gluing an area and applying one color at a time until the picture is complete.

❶-❸

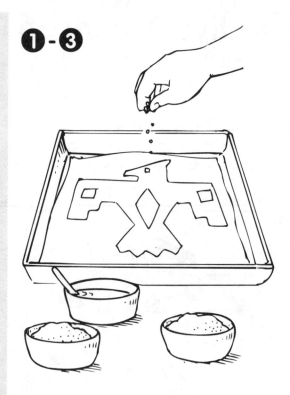

❹

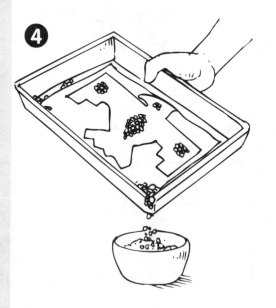

Holiday Fun • EMC 742

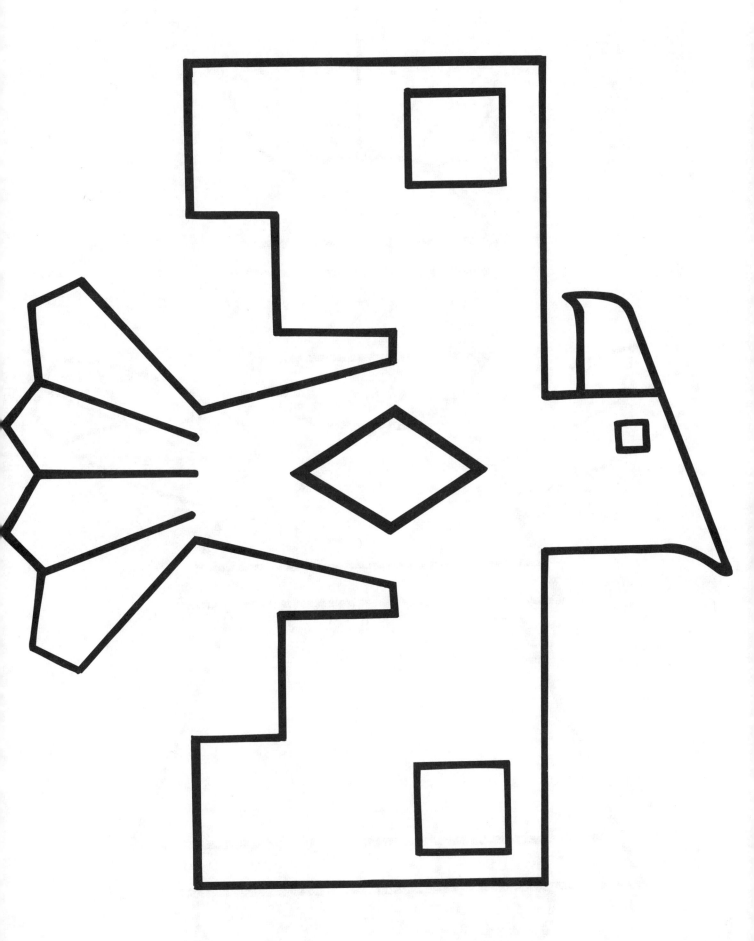

★ Stick Dice Game

These simple dice were used in a gambling game played by many Native American tribes. As children enjoy this game, they will be utilizing the math skills of counting and adding and will be introduced to the concept of probability.

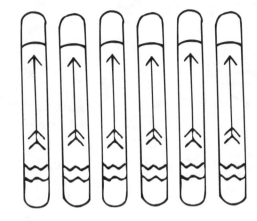

This is a game for 2 or more players. Only one set of sticks is needed for each game.

If you divide the class into small playing groups, each child can make two or three of the "dice" needed for the group. Each group will need to decide cooperatively on the design pattern for their sticks so that all six sticks look similar.

Materials:
- 6 tongue depressors
- marking pens
- paper and pencil to keep score

Have students decorate *only one side* of each stick.

Game rules:
The object of the game is to be the first player to reach 5 points. (A higher point total may be set for older students.)

Scoring is as follows:

All six sticks face up or all face down	= 2 points.	
Three up and three down	= 1 point.	
All other combinations	= 0 points.	

How to Play

1. The first player holds the sticks loosely in one hand, and taps them on the table while chanting for luck:

Hey chin-a-ma
Hey chin-a-ma
Hoya, hoya, hey!

2. The player drops the sticks.
3. The player tallies the score.
4. Play passes to the player on the left.
5. Play continues until one player reaches 5 points.

⭐ Indian Vests

These easy-to-make vests require only paper grocery bags, tempera paints, and scissors.

Teacher preparation:

❶ Cut down center on one wide side.

❷ Cut an opening for the child's head on the bottom of the bag.

❸ Cut out arm holes on both narrow sides.

Student steps:

❶ Cut the lower edge of the vest into vertical strips, creating fringe.

❷ Use tempera paints to add designs to the vest. Dry thoroughly before wearing.

⭐ Indian Capes

Materials:
- wide butcher paper
- scissors
- paints or marking pens

Steps to follow:

❶ Draw a large circle on the butcher paper.

❷ Students cut from the outside edge to the circle and then cut out the circle.

❸ Paint or color designs on the cape.

❹ Fringe edge of cape.

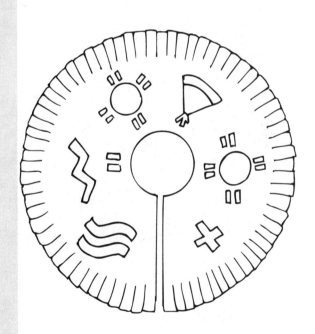

Indian Beads

Materials:
- dried pasta—any shape with a hole in the center
- food colorings
- alcohol
- zipper-lock plastic bags, large
- string

Coloring pasta:
1. Place 1 pound of uncooked pasta in large plastic zipper-lock bag.
2. Add 2–3 tablespoons of rubbing alcohol and 5-15 drops of food coloring.
3. Zip bag and shake until color is even.
4. Spread out on newspaper to dry.
5. Make a variety of colors and store each in a separate bag.

Stringing the beads:
1. Wrap a piece of masking tape around the end of the string to stiffen it, making it easier for small fingers to control.
2. String the pasta to create a necklace of brightly colored "beads." Encourage children to create a pattern.

Let children share their necklaces with the class and explain the patterns used. You may want to help the children name the patterns—ABCABC, ABBABB, etc.

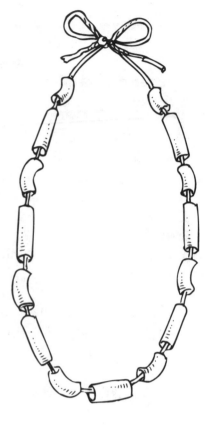

 Indian Headbands

Materials:
- sentence strips
- burlap or imitation suede fabric, cut to fit sentence strips
- felt, cut in shapes of the patterns on page 79
- glue
- scissors

Steps to follow:
1. Prepare headbands by gluing burlap or imitation suede to sentence strips.
2. Allow students to glue felt designs on the headband. If desired, ask students to create a pattern.
3. When glue is dry, staple headbands to fit.

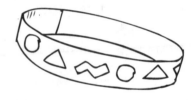

 Indian Arm Cuffs

Reproduce the pattern on page 80 for each student.
Allow students to color the designs with crayons. Then cut on the dotted lines, creating fringe. Roll each cuff around wrist and tape or staple in place.

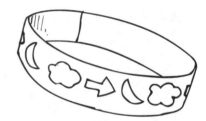

mountain

sun

arrow

lightning

cloud

snake/water

moon

diamond

bear track

Holiday Fun • EMC 742

★ Medicine Pouch

Many Native American groups used medicine pouches made of animal skin to carry items of special significance. These items might have included objects for health or luck in warfare, such as herbs, small carved rocks, or pieces of antler, shell, or bone.

Children, being natural collectors, will enjoy making and filling their own "medicine pouches."

Materials:
- 12" (30.5 cm) square of brown craft paper (A square cut from a grocery bag is ideal.)
- string or raffia
- crayons

Steps to follow:
❶ Draw "Native American" designs on the brown paper.

❷ Crush, crumple, and rub paper until it becomes very crinkled and soft.

❸ Children place their special items in the center, pull up the edges of paper, and tie with string or raffia.

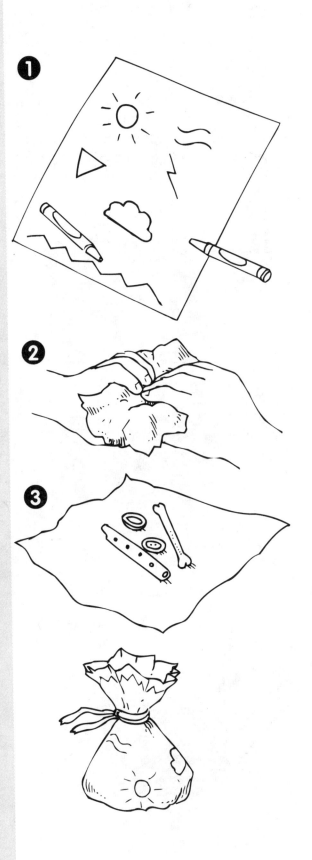

Holiday Fun • EMC 742

Columbus Day

Christopher Columbus may not have been the first European to travel to the American continents, but his efforts did open the New World to exploration and settlement. In August of 1492, he set sail from Spain with 120 men in three small ships, the Nina, the Pinta, and the Santa Maria. On October 12, the ships landed in the Bahamas.

①

②

③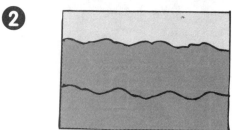

④⑤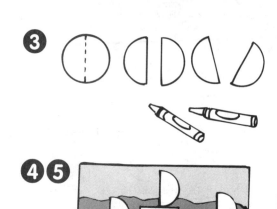

Make a collage picture of Columbus's voyage.

Materials:
- 3-4" circles cut from manilla paper
- 9" x 12" (23 X 30.5 cm) dark blue construction paper
- 9" x 12" (23 X 30.5 cm) light blue construction paper
- scissors
- crayons or markers
- glue

Steps to follow:

❶ Demonstrate for children how to cut in a wavy line at about the mid-point of the dark blue paper. This is the "ocean."

❷ Overlap the "ocean" pieces and glue to the bottom of the light blue paper.

❸ Cut circles in half. Color three half-circles to create the hulls of the boats.

❹ Glue together as pictured to make boats with sails.

❺ Glue boats on the "waves." You might want to place one or two boats so that the lower wave covers part of the hull.

Halloween

Halloween in the United States is celebrated as a fun day for children to dress up and enjoy spooky fun. Pages 83–91 present seven activities from art to snacks to finger plays to add variety to your Halloween fun.

Here are some great Halloween stories to share any time during the Halloween season:
Scary, Scary Halloween by Eve Bunting; Scholastic, 1986.
Pumpkin, Pumpkin by Jeanne Titherington; Scholastic, 1986.
Space Case by Edward Marshall; Dial Press, 1982.

 ## ★ Crispy Jack o' Lantern Tortillas

Materials:
- flour tortillas
- plastic knives
- salad oil
- electric frying pan
- cinnamon
- sugar
- napkins or paper towels

How to make:

❶ Give each child a flour tortilla and a small plastic knife.

❷ Allow children to cut a jack o' lantern face in the tortilla.

❸ Fry each tortilla in a little bit of oil, using an electric skillet. Make sure children stay well back from skillet, in case of splattering. You will want to have a parent or aide on hand to help.

❹ Remove tortilla from skillet and immediately sprinkle with a mixture of cinnamon and sugar.

❺ Let cool briefly and serve.

Find the Witch's Cat

Children love this flannel board activity because of the fun characters and the opportunity it gives them to use their powers of observation and deduction.

Reproduce the patterns on pages 85-88 on heavy paper or tagboard. Color, cut out, and attach a Velcro® strip to the back.

Position the objects on the flannel board. Turn the flannel board toward you and secretly hide the cat under one of the objects.

Say to the group, "The witch has lost her cat. Let's help her find it."

Teach the children the following chant. Use "witchy" voices to add to the fun!

> **Come my pretty,**
> **Come my pet,**
> **You can't hide**
> **I'll find you yet!**

Choose a child to come up and say where he/she thinks the cat is hiding. Then, let him/her check the guess. If correct, he/she hides the cat and calls on the group. If incorrect, he/she chooses the next guesser.

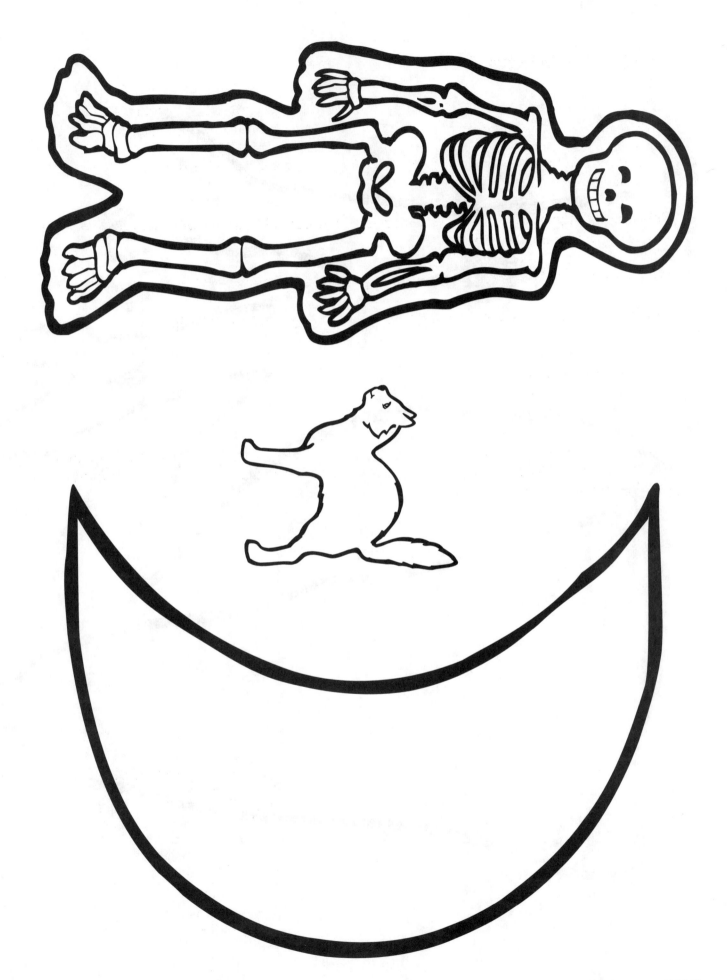

85

Holiday Fun • EMC 742

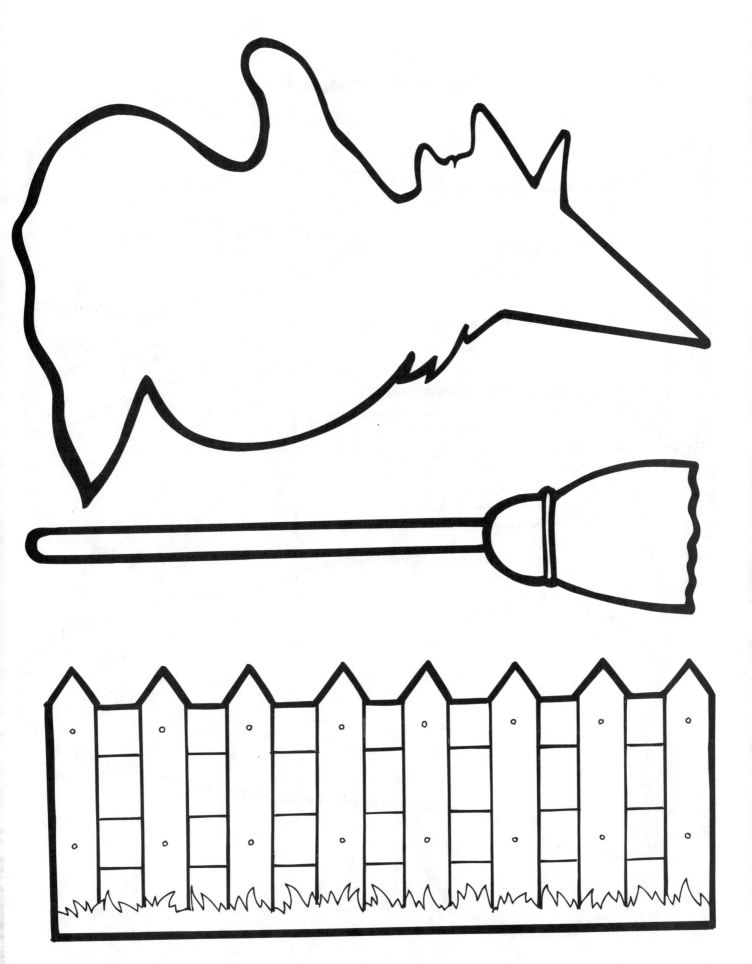

Holiday Fun • EMC 742

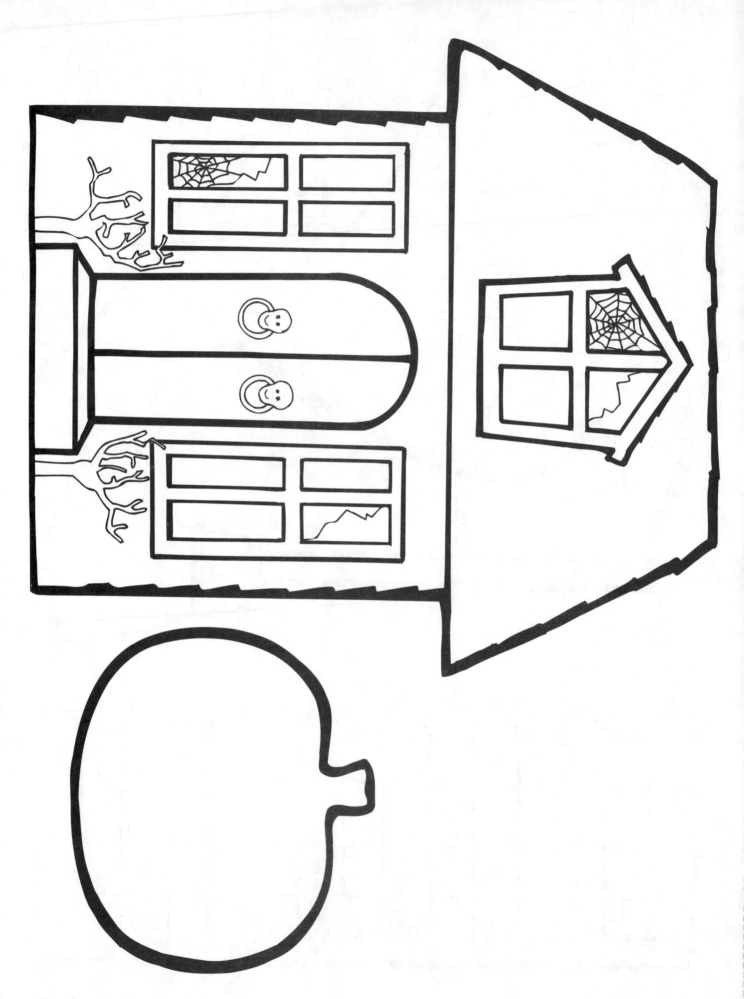

⭐ Finger Plays and Chants

Wide-Eyed Owl

This finger play is sure to be a favorite at Halloween and all year round.

There's a wide-eyed owl	(Make circles around eyes, with index finger and thumb)
With a pointed nose	(Join index fingers over nose, forming beak)
Two pointed ears	(Use fingers to make pointy "ears" on top of head)
And claws for his toes.	(Bend fingers of both hands to make claws)
He lives high in a tree	(Point up high)
And when he looks at you	(Point to someone)
He flaps his wings	(Place hands at underarms and flap elbows)
And he says "Whoo! Whoo!"	

Stirring My Brew

This is sure to be the favorite Halloween activity of many of your students!

Form a circle. Tell the children that the center of the circle is the "cauldron." Chant in a singsong manner.

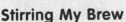

Stirring and stirring and stirring our brew	(Everyone pretends to stir)
Ooo-oo-ooo, ooo-oo-ooo,	(A ghostly, haunting sound)
Stirring and stirring and stirring our brew	(Everyone pretends to stir)
Tiptoe, tiptoe, tiptoe	(Everyone takes tiny tiptoe steps toward center of circle)

(Pause for a moment and then shout)

BOO!

Halloween Cat

Here is another singsong chant.

> *Halloween cat*
> *Halloween cat*
> *Why do you yowl and howl like that?*
> *Neither I nor the moon*
> *Like your tune.*
> *Scat! (shout) Halloween cat!*

Holiday Fun • EMC 742

Owl Drawing

This cute owl is easy and fun. Have children work on light brown construction paper and tell them to fill the page, so you have nice big owls to decorate your classroom.

Here are the steps to follow.

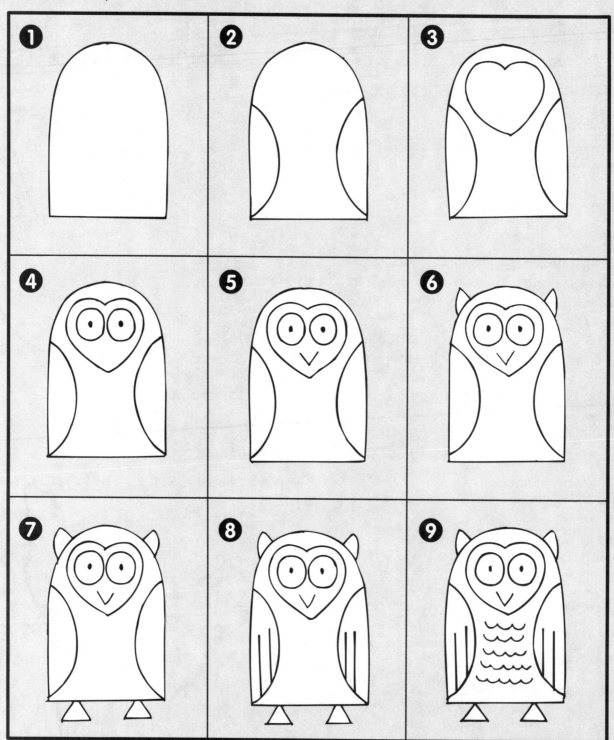

Allow students to use colored chalk to add color and detail.

90   Holiday Fun • EMC 742

Black Cat

This nifty black cat gives little hands practice at cutting and always turns out great.

Materials:
- 9" x 12" (23 x 30.5 cm) black construction paper
- white crayon
- scissors
- glue

Steps to follow:

❶ Draw lines on black construction paper with white crayon as shown. (This is a great "take home" job for a parent volunteer.)

❷ Students cut on the white lines.

❸ Show students how to accordion-fold the tail back and forth to add dimension.

❹ Glue head and tail to body as shown.

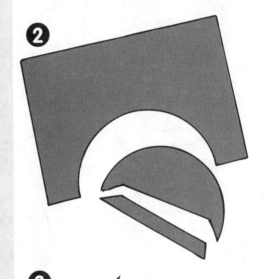

Diwali

This is a happy, cheerful occasion in India. It is a celebration of Lakshmi, the goddess of wealth and prosperity. Indians clean and decorate their homes and make good luck designs with rice flour on the floor near the entrances to their homes. In hope that Lakshmi will bless their homes, Indians make clay lamps to guide her.

★ Diwali Lamps

Materials:
- self-hardening clay
- tempera or acrylic paint
- paintbrushes
- small candles

Steps to follow:

❶ Give each child a fist-sized ball of clay.

❷ Show children how to pinch clay into a shallow bowl shape.

❸ Let dry. Paint as desired. Geometric designs in earth colors are traditional.

❹ Place a candle in center of bowl using a base of soft clay.

Veteran's Day

Veteran's Day, also known as Armistice Day, is the day set aside to honor all those who have served in the United States armed services. Any person who has served in the armed forces is called a veteran. On this day we express our appreciation for the many sacrifices made by veterans to protect our country.

★ Thank You Banner

Make a large banner to display outside your school or to deliver to a veterans' hospital or VFW Post in your community. Also, any retirement or nursing home is sure to house veterans who would very much appreciate being remembered.

Materials:
- butcher paper
- tempera paint
- crepe paper streamers in red, white, and blue

Steps to follow:

❶ Paint the words, "Thank You Veterans" in the center of the butcher paper.

❷ Allow children to paint hearts, stars, and other designs around the words. They might sign their names as well.

❸ Make bows from the crepe paper streamers and attach them to the banner.

Thanksgiving

The pilgrims who came to America from England in 1620 faced many hardships and dangers. After their first good harvest, their leader, Governor Bradford, declared a three-day feast of Thanksgiving to God. This important tradition has been cherished through the years and is considered the most American of all holidays.

Read **The Thanksgiving Story** by Alice Dalgliesh (Scholastic, 1990).

★ Friendship Vegetable Soup

Sharing good food has always been central to Thanksgiving. Create a warm and delicious soup to share as you celebrate this delightful day. Ask a few parents to come in and help.

Materials:
- safety knives
- paper plates
- soup bowls and spoons
- vegetables
- canned chicken or vegetable broth
- canned tomatoes
- salt & pepper

Steps to follow:

❶ Ask each student to bring in a vegetable.

❷ Allow students to wash and cut up their vegetables.

❸ Place all cut up vegetables in a soup pot with the tomatoes and broth.

❹ Bring to a simmer and cook until all vegetables are tender.

❺ Add salt and pepper to taste.

★ Pilgrim Costumes

A Thanksgiving play or feast in your classroom would be incomplete without these simple pilgrim costumes.

Girl Pilgrim Bonnet

Materials:
- 12" x 18" (30.5 x 45.5 cm) white construction paper
- scissors
- 2 - 8" (20 cm) pieces of yarn or roving
- stapler
- hole punch

Steps to follow:

❶ Fold back 3" (7.5 cm) on one long side.

❷ Cut 2 triangles out of paper as shown.

❸ Fold section B down.

❹ Fold A and C across B and staple each in place.

❺ Punch holes in both corners of the front fold. Tie a piece of yarn through each hole.

❻ Place on head and tie in place.

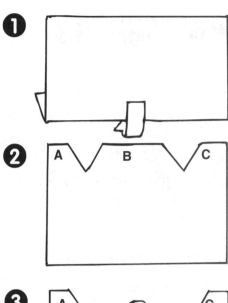

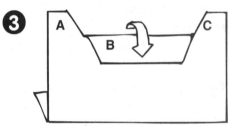

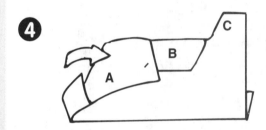

Holiday Fun • EMC 742

Boy Pilgrim Hat

Materials:
- sentence strips
- tagboard templates made from patterns on page 97
- 9" x 12" (23 x 30.5 cm) black construction paper
- 2 1/2" x 3" (6.25 x 7.5 cm) yellow construction paper
- scissors
- glue
- stapler

Steps to follow:

❶ To make a base for the hat, measure a sentence strip to fit each child's head. Staple.

❷ Trace hat template on black paper and cut out.

❸ Staple the bottom edge of the hat piece to the sentence strip.

❹ Trace the buckle template on yellow construction paper and cut out.

❺ Glue buckle to hat.

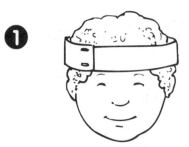

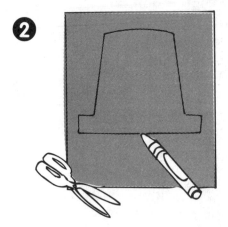

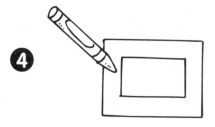

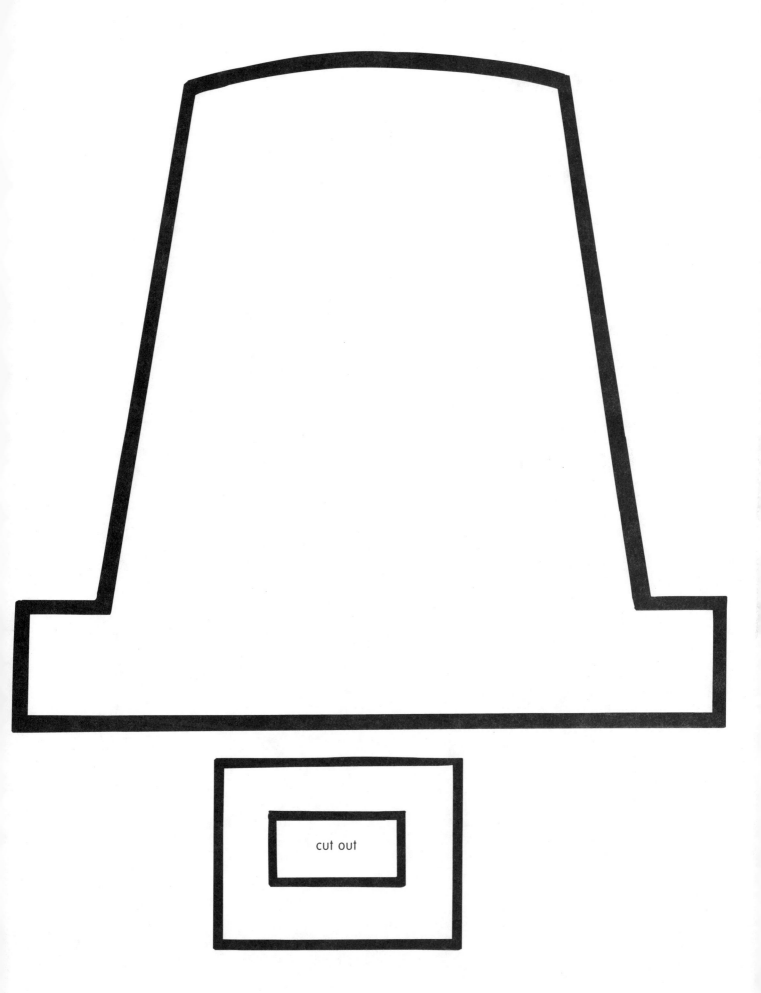

cut out

⭐ Collar for Boys and Girls

Materials:
- 12" x 18" (30.5 x 45.5 cm) white construction paper
- 2 - 10" (25.5 cm) pieces of yarn or roving

Steps to follow:

❶ Fold paper in half lengthwise.

❷ Fold paper in half crosswise.

❸ Open crosswise fold. Cut a half-circle centered on crosswise fold to create neck opening.

❹ Open paper and cut up one crosswise fold to open collar.

❺ Punch holes at points marked "X."

❻ Tie a 10" piece of yarn in each of the holes.

❼ Place collar over child's shoulders and tie in front.

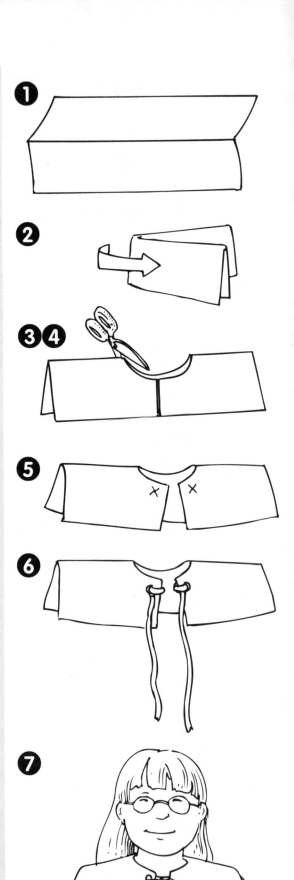

Holiday Fun • EMC 742

Dried Plant Centerpiece

This is a beautiful project that can be successfully completed by children of any age. The results are always wonderful.

Start in September asking parents and any avid gardeners you know to send cuttings that you can dry.

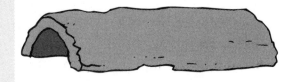

Materials:
- chunks of bark at least 6" x 12" (15 x 30.5 cm) OR
- rough rounds with bark cut from tree trunks or limbs at least 8" in diameter
- florists' clay
- white glue
- large variety of dried plants with seed pods. Look for a variety of heights, shapes, and textures. Store-bought dried flowers and wheat may be added.

Steps to follow:

❶ Glue a 3" ball of moist clay in the center of the bark base.

❷ Let children select plants and arrange them on the base by sticking the stems into the clay.

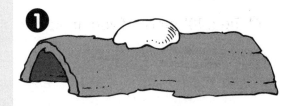

Things I'm Thankful For

At this time of year, it is valuable to reflect on all the reasons we have to be thankful. Make a colorful class book based on this theme.

Brainstorm together about all the things you and the students are thankful for. Write each idea on a long edge of a 9" x 12" (23 x 30.5 cm) sheet of drawing paper.

Each child chooses one idea to illustrate, using crayons or markers.

To make a cover for the book, reproduce the pattern on page 101 on light-colored construction paper.

Add a back cover, hole punch all pages, and bind with roving in a contrasting color.

There's a wonderful song called "Things I'm Thankful For." You can find it on the recording ***Ideas, Thoughts, and Feelings*** by Hap Palmer, Activity Records.

We Are Thankful...

Holiday Fun • EMC 742

Hanukkah - Festival of Lights

Hanukkah commemorates a time when the Jewish people in Israel were battling for religious freedom. They had recaptured their temple and were preparing to give thanks. They lit the temple lamp, and although they had only enough oil for one day, the lamp miraculously burned for eight days. Today families light the Menorah in remembrance of the miracle and share special foods, games, and gifts.

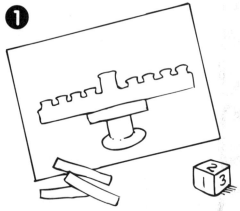

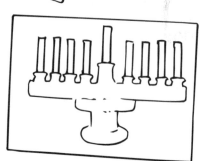

★ Literature Connection

Share this truly delightful Hanukkah story with your class:

The Chanukah Guest by Eric A. Kimmel (Scholastic, 1988).

Make latkes like the ones in the story using this simple recipe. Serve the latkes with applesauce and sour cream.

- 4 cups grated potatoes
- 4 eggs
- 1/4 cup matzo meal
- 2 teaspoons salt
- vegetable oil

Mix all ingredients. Drop spoonfuls of the mixture onto a skillet or griddle coated with hot oil, forming small pancakes about 3" in diameter. Brown on both sides. Makes about 2 dozen.

★ The Menorah Game

Materials:
- Menorah pattern on page 103 for each child
- 9 - 1/2" x 2" (1.25 x 5 cm) strips of yellow construction paper per child to represent candles
- One die for every 2 players. Place masking tape over each face of a die. Mark 2 sides of the die with each of these numbers: 1, 2, 3.

How to play:
❶ Children work with a partner. Take turns rolling the die. Each time a player rolls, he/she may place that number of candles on his/her menorah.
❷ The object is to be the first to fill in the menorah, using the exact roll of the die.

©1998 by Evan-Moor Corp.Holiday Fun • EMC 742

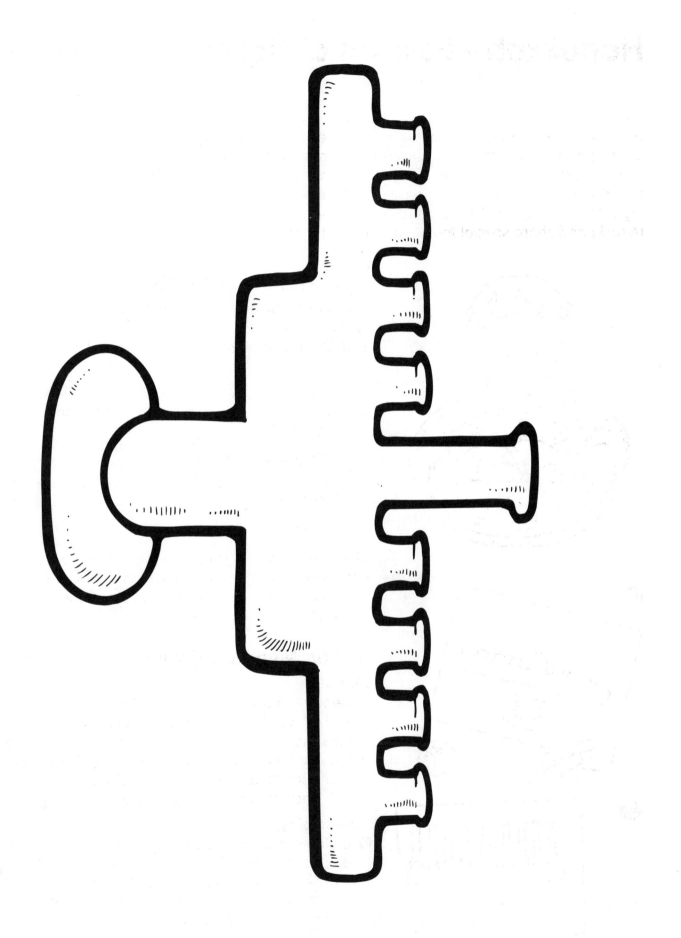

⭐ The Dreidel Game

A dreidel is a four-sided top used to play a game that has been a Hanukkah tradition for hundreds of years. Here is an easy way to make dreidels so that your class can enjoy playing the game.

How to make:

1. Cut a 3" square out of tagboard for each dreidel.

2. Reproduce and cut out the patterns shown. Glue to tagboard square.

   Note: the Hebrew letters represent a phrase meaning, "A great miracle happened there."

3. Punch a hole in the center of the square. Push a short pencil through the hole.

How to play:

1. Give each player an equal supply of tokens. Foil-wrapped chocolate coins are traditional, but raisins or peanuts work well.

2. Each player puts 2 tokens into the "pot."

3. The first player spins and takes the action indicated on the side of the dreidel that lands down on the playing surface.
   Gimel - take everything in the pot.
   Hey - take half of the pot.
   Shin - put one token in the pot.
   Nun - take nothing.

4. Each player puts another token in the "pot" and the next player takes a turn.

5. Play continues until each player has taken 4 turns. The player with the most coins wins.

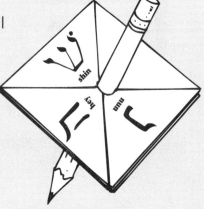

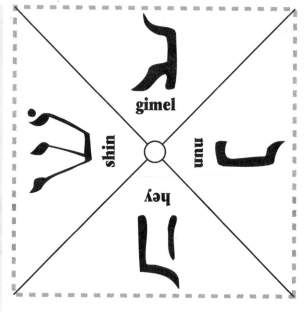

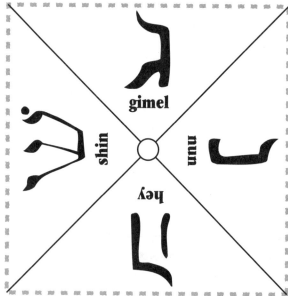

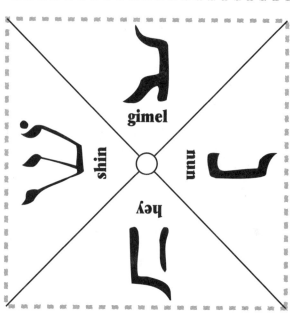

Christmas

Christmas is an important day for Christians worldwide. It is the day set aside to celebrate the birth of Jesus which occurred about 2000 years ago. Many Christmas customs are based on the story of the nativity. Gifts are exchanged on this day in remembrance of gifts the three wise men gave to the Christ child. Homes are decorated with lights to symbolize the light that shone over the stable where Jesus was born. Families, churches, and communities display nativity scenes.

A sweet and age-appropriate book to share with your class is **The First Noel** by B.G. Hennessey (Scholastic, 1993).

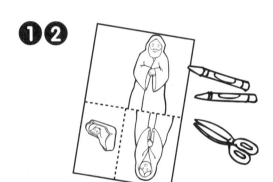

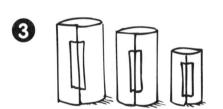

★ A Simple Nativity Scene

Materials:
- patterns on page 106, reproduced on fairly heavy paper
- scissors
- crayons
- cellophane tape

Steps to follow:

❶ Cut the patterns apart on the dotted lines.

❷ Color each character.

❸ Help children roll each section into a tube and secure with tape on the back.

❹ Stand tubes together on a table or shelf.

❺ Add straw and small plastic barnyard animals to complete the scene.

Holiday Fun • EMC 742

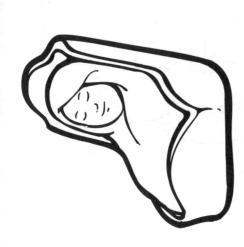

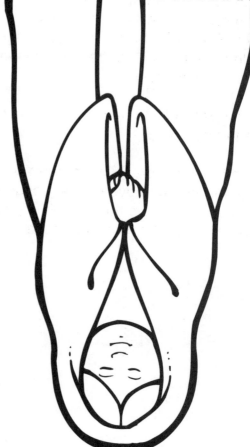

106

⭐ Epsom Salts "Frost" Painting

The fanciful technique described below can be used to create a snowy Christmas picture or winter scene.

Materials:
- tagboard templates made from patterns on page 108
- 9" x 12" (23 x 30.5 cm) blue construction paper
- 4" x 5" (10 x 13 cm) scraps of colored construction paper
- glue
- paintbrush
- Epsom salts mixture (Prepare ahead)

1. Mix 2 cups Epsom salts with 1 cup water in saucepan.
2. Heat and stir until dissolved.
3. Keep warm (not hot) on a hot plate.

Steps to follow:

❶ Trace shapes onto construction paper using templates. Cut out.

❷ Arrange the shapes on the blue paper to create a pleasing scene. Encourage individuality of expression. For example, some children may want to do an entire forest of evergreens, others may want a line of snowmen.

❸ Glue the shapes to the blue construction paper. Set aside to dry.

❹ Use a paintbrush to spread warm epsom salts mixture generously and evenly over collage pictures. The Epsom salts mixture will crystallize as it dries, lending a frosty appearance.

108

Kwanzaa

Kwanzaa is a new holiday in which many African-American people celebrate African customs and traditions. Emphasis is placed on family and positive values. Homes are decorated with straw mats, ears of corn, and a kinara, which is a special holder for seven candles. One candle is lit for each day of the celebration. Families exchange homemade gifts and enjoy being together. On the last day there is a feast, music, and dancing.

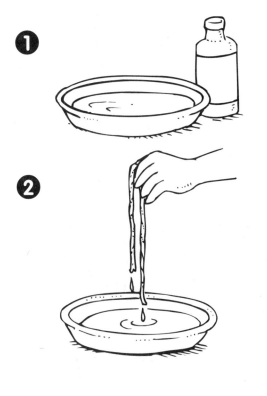

★ Napkin Rings

These make wonderful homemade gifts for the whole family, and add a beautiful touch to the Kwanzaa table.

Materials:
- paper towel tubes, cut into 2" (5 cm) lengths
- 18" (45.5 cm) lengths of yarn or roving in bright colors
- liquid starch
- pie plates
- waxed paper

Steps to follow:

❶ Pour liquid starch into pie plates or similar shallow dishes.

❷ Dip yarn into starch mixture and then hold yarn above dish for a few seconds, allowing excess starch to drain away.

❸ Wrap yarn around paper tube as shown.

❹ Use any combination of colors, continuing to wrap cores with yarn until the tube is completely covered. Set to dry on waxed paper.

⭐ The Kinara

The kinara is the special holder of seven candles used to celebrate Kwanzaa. The candles represent the seven principles of Kwanzaa—unity, self-determination, collective work and responsibility, cooperative economics, purpose, creativity, and faith. The corn is an important Kwanzaa symbol that stands for children in a family.

This simple project makes an attractive decoration.

Materials:
- 12" x 18" (30.5 x 45.5) blue construction paper
- 7 - 2" (5 cm) squares of white construction paper
- 1/2" x 2" (1.25 x 5 cm) strips for candles, each child needs 3 red, 3 green, 1 black
- small pieces of yellow tissue paper
- 2 - 2" x 4" (5 x 10 cm) manilla paper
- tempera paints in yellow, red, and orange
- pie tins
- dried corn husks (available in the Mexican food or produce section of your market)
- glue
- scissors

Steps to follow:
❶ Show children how to glue white squares to the blue paper in a stairstep pattern. Adult help will likely be needed to correctly place the top center square.

❷ Glue on "candles"—red on left, green on right, black in center.

❸ Glue on torn bits of tissue for flames.

❹ Cut oval corn cobs from manilla paper.

❺ Pour a thin layer of tempera paint into pie plates. Show children how to dip a finger into the paint and print "kernels" all over corn cobs.

❻ Glue corn cobs to the background and add several pieces of corn husk for an authentic look.

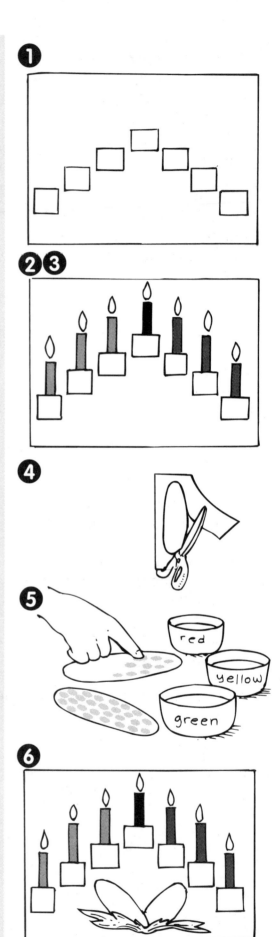

★ Andinkera Cloth

Andinkera cloth is a beautiful, colorful cloth covered with repeating designs. It was named for an African King and can be used to make clothing, wall hangings, or pillows.

Materials:
- muslin, any color
- large potatoes, cut in half crosswise
- patterns on page 112
- acrylic paints
- pie plates
- masking tape
- paring knife

Steps to follow:
By an adult -
❶ Cut or tear muslin into 24" (61 cm) squares.

❷ Tape each square to a table top, stretching slightly.

❸ Use a pencil to draw a simple design on the cut surface of each potato half. If you use the patterns on page 112, lay the pattern on the potato and trace over the lines with a pencil pressing hard enough to imprint the design on the potato.

❹ Use a paring knife to cut away excess potato around the design.

❺ Spread a thin layer of paint in the bottom of each pie plate.

By children -
Instruct children to dip potato into paint and stamp onto fabric to create a pattern.

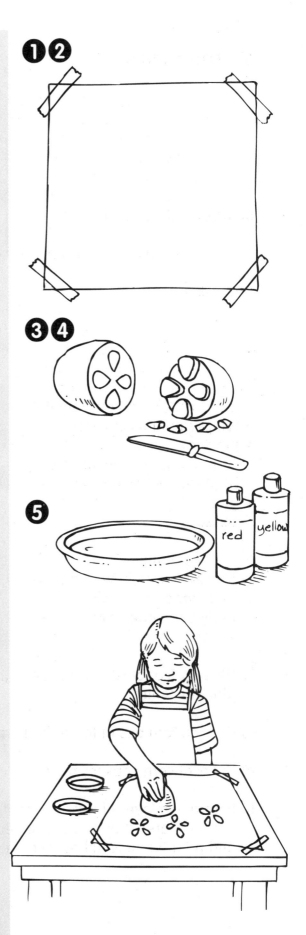

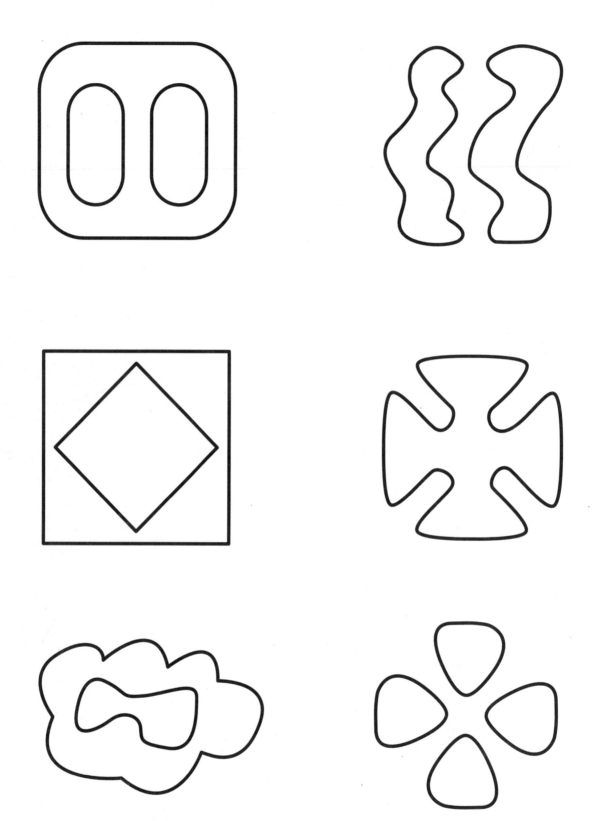

Holiday Fun • EMC 742